Recruitment
101
9-5 Employment Tips

Dr. Arthur Johnson (PsyD)

Contents

Chapter 1:
Meaning and Scope of Recruitment

Meaning of Recruitment

Human resources are fundamental to an organization's performance. Consequently, effective employee recruitment plays a crucial role, directly impacting both the organization's success and its long-term survival. The street or layman meaning of recruitment is employment. To the ordinary person, recruitment is giving an opportunity to some persons or groups of persons to be involved in a phenomenon, activity, or decision-making. This simply denotes the inclusion of new person or groups of people into a group or society. Hence, ecology defines recruitment as the increase in natural population as offspring grow and new members arrive. In human studies, recruitment can also be defined as the act of enlisting new people into an office or organization. The security services, such as the military, police, immigration, fire, and prison services, normally use the term enlistment. In another sense, recruitment is also explained as the process of finding, attracting, and involving potential (human) resources for a specific position or job in an organization. It denotes filling vacant positions in an organization and involves the hiring process, from inception to the individual recruit's integration into the company. Recruitment is the process of locating, sourcing, screening, shortlisting, interviewing, and ultimately hiring or onboarding qualified candidates for job openings. Simply, recruitment is done to choose qualified people to fill a vacant space in an organization.

Processes Involved in Recruitment

Despite its importance, recruiting people into an organization is challenging for most organizations because organizations and employment seekers have different needs. Balancing the two interests requires a multilevel structure that demonstrates the interplay between organizational-level factors and individual-level factors. Many organizations prefer to outsource their recruitment processes to external firms. This is largely due to the complex structure required to address both organizational and job seeker needs, as well as the demanding nature of recruitment itself. Outsourcing allows companies to leverage the expertise and personnel of specialized organizations to manage these functions effectively. Others also choose to equip the organization's human resource wing to handle the task internally. Recruitment is a process. It goes through a systematic way before the best-qualified candidate is selected. The timeline for recruitment is subjective, depending on an organization's specifications and ideals for recruitment and job specifications. In some instances, the recruitment process takes a few to several months. In other instances, it is relatively short and takes a few days and even hours. While some job seekers are given instant employment after the interview, others take some time before the preferred candidate is called. The recruitment process simply denotes the ways used to identify vacancies (job specifics), analyze job requirement(s), review applications, and shortlist and select the right candidate to fill a vacant position in an organization. The processes involved in recruitment include recruitment planning, identifying vacancies, declaring vacant positions, finding prospective job seekers, screening and shortlisting prospective job seekers, interviewing prospective job seekers, reviewing interviewees, and finally, hiring and onboarding job seekers.

Recruitment Planning

One basic requirement in the recruitment process is planning. It is the first step of the recruitment process in which vacancies, job specifications, qualifications, competencies, remuneration, other conditions of service, and other modules for the office created are thoroughly discussed. As the foundation step, the rest of the process is hinged on the planning. Every step, action, and decision of the recruitment process needs to be planned well before the other steps follow. If the planning of the recruitment process goes wrong, most of the activities in the process may follow suit. That is one reason why it normally needs experts to handle the planning of the recruitment process for an organization. Recruitment planning involves identifying vacant positions, identifying job analysis, spelling out work descriptions and work specifications, and doing work evaluations. It also involves working on other processes such as identifying vacancies, declaring vacant positions, finding prospective job seekers, screening job seekers, shortlisting prospective job seekers, interviewing prospective job seekers, sieving prospective job seekers, and finally hiring and onboarding job seekers. Identifying vacant positions in an organization is the initial stage in planning. The identification of vacancies includes a number of positions that need to be filled. The number of employees a company needs at a particular time depends on several factors. Consequently, while new jobs might need a whole team or a quite number of people to fill almost every position created, current organizations need few people to fill spaces that are created due to death, resignation, retirement, or sacking of the officer that manned the position. Identification also includes a job description. This involves identifying the ranks that need to be filled. Determining whether an organization needs senior or junior staff, experts or lay workers, or skill-based or academic-based personnel are all important for the success of the process. It also involves job description, which includes expression of the location of the organization, what the organization does, its core values, mission and vision statements, and prospects. The next step is the responsibilities expected by the personnel to fill those positions. Vividly describing the roles of the person(s) needed for employment in an organization is very crucial. Because organizations need to maximize profit while cutting costs, it is important to employ people who shall not just add up to the numbers in the officers but actually be productive. Thus, job roles should clearly be spelled out for the vacant position identified. The tenure of office for the personnel going to manage the vacant position is also as crucial as the rest. Whether permanent or temporary, the tenure should be clearly stated so that job seekers know what is in for them before they apply. The tenure also includes whether the job in question is a full-time or part-time session. The qualifications and experiences one needs to have in order to be eligible for that position should also be clearly stated. This shall make only qualified people apply for the position. This helps in the selection process. Planning also involves job evaluation. Other scholars also refer to this as job analysis or grading. It is the comparative analysis of the job in question in relation to other similar positions, either in the same organization or in other organizations. After all these steps are done, a company is then deemed ready to declare vacant positions and advertise them publicly.

Declaring Vacant Positions

Declaring a vacant position in an organization follows the identification stage. Until this is done, an organization is seen to have reached its equilibrium in terms of the ratio between staff and work. Prospective job seekers usually would not worry themselves writing application letters to such organizations that have not declared any vacancies. Some curious prospective employees may reach out to contacts within the organization to inquire about potential job openings. Once a position is declared vacant, the process of finding a suitable candidate to fill that role begins.

Finding Prospective Job Seekers

Many organizations have regretted employing one person or the other once in a while. A wrong choice might mar whatever achievement the organization has fulfilled and might even contribute to its collapse. Finding the right candidate for a vacant position in an organization is task-involving. It needs due diligence, tact, and a sense of reasoning to do a successful and impactful search for an organization. Finding prospective job applicants is also referred to as sourcing. Prospective vacant position filler can be selected from two main sources: internal source or external source. Internal source recruitment includes mainly promotions and transfers. External sources of recruitment include direct recruitment, employee exchanges, employment agencies, advertisements, professional associations, campus recruitment, word of mouth of former employees, employee referrals, and previous applicants.

Screening and Shortlisting Job Seekers

Screening commences after sourcing candidates. Screening is described as the process of filtering or sieving the applications for further selection. The screening process involves the review of application letters or cover letters, résumés or curriculum vitae, and other attached particulars, such as birth certificates, educational and professional certificates, and National Service Certificates (as pertaining to Ghana and other West African countries), among others. With regards to professional organizations, additional certificates such as licensure are reviewed. During the screening session, issues such as reasons for leaving a previous job (if any), reasons for applying for the job, long unemployment rate, and career progression are looked at. In some organizations, especially law firms, consultancy firms, and communication organizations, things like spelling, addresses, referees, arrangement, wording of the curriculum vitae or profile, and expressions are all looked at. Some companies can disqualify applicants for a petty mistake in spelling, citing the absence of due diligence and proofreading as the basis. Only the shortlisted applicants are allowed to go to the next stage of the recruitment process. The applicants are invited through phone calls, letters, text messages, emails, or any other means available or as stated by the applicant. Screening helps remove unqualified and false candidates who were overlooked at the sourcing stage. It also helps to reduce the number of applicants to the most qualified ones, which makes interviews very easy and time-saving.

Interviewing Prospective Job Seekers

Interviews are scheduled for qualified job applicants after screening and shortlisting. Only the shortlisted applicants are invited after screening. Interview dates, times, venues, and other important things are stated in the information sent to the applicant ahead of the interview. This makes room for adequate preparation, which includes information finding and finding modes of transport and accommodation if the organization is not in the vicinity of applicants. Two forms of interviews exist. One is the one-on-one or face-to-face interview. This type of interview requires the applicant to be present in person at the venue. This type of interview allows the panel and organization to observe applicants' physical attributes and gain insights into their character, which may not be as evident in other types of interviews. Another form of interview is the telephone interview. With this type of interview, applicants are interviewed on telephone and need not to be physically present at any venue. The telephone interview can make an applicant conceal some personal attributes. An applicant can use a book to answer professional or technical questions, and the interviewer will not know. The applicant might even ask another person to do the interview, and no one will know. Modernity has brought a new form of interview, which is video calls. With this type, there is a video session with the help of modern apps, such as Zoom Meeting, WhatsApp, Facebook Messenger, or Telegram, that allows the interviewer to see the applicant being interviewed. Interviews can take any form. There are no clear-cut rules or forms for it. However, most interview sessions concentrate on experience, past jobs, reasons for leaving former organizations, expected salary, and courses. Other interviewers can cynically veer into unconventional themes, such as family life, politics, and religion, among others. Interviews can be short or drag. It can be exciting or exhaustive, too. While most interviews involve a conversation, some interviews might also include a written examination. Some can even involve reviewing videos, short films, symbols, or pictures, depending on the job description. In line with this, one cannot prepare enough for a particular interview or perfectly answer all the questions during the interview session.

Reviewing Interview Performance

The next stage after interviewing applicants is to review the performance of the applicants. Some organizations can have marathon interviews and reviews in a day until the qualified applicant is picked. Other organizations schedule different dates for follow-up interviews for qualified applicants from the first interviews. This is especially done for top positions and technical positions that need a critical review of applicants' performance during the interview session. The criteria for scoring applicants during interviews differ from organization to organization and from region to region. Conventionally, most organizations look at the accuracy of responses or answers, timing, reasoning power, personality, dress code, confidence level, and posture during the interview session. Some panel members can fail an applicant based on how they knocked on the door to the interview room, how an applicant opened the door to the interview room without hearing any response after knocking, or even how an applicant walked to their seat. One of the troubling and stress-filled times in a person's life is the review of a job interview session one attended. Anxiety makes many people do funny things. But it is part of the process and should be done. After reviews, only applicants who performed excellently are selected for another interview session (when most applicants did well and the best-performing applicants surpass the number needed for the job). Most often, the best-performing applicant is called, written to, or sent a message that they have been recruited because they excelled in the interview. Notwithstanding this rigorous process, many job seekers believe that the recruitment process, from the start to the interview session, is a scam and depends on flimsy factors, such as whom you know (or currently, who knows you), parental affiliation to bosses in the organization, beauty or handsomeness, or coincidental factors like same name, tribe, race, religion, or same former school. Many young job seekers lack trust in the recruitment process and often dislike it when a recruitment agency handles it.

Hiring and Onboarding Job Seekers

Hiring and onboarding is the final stage in the recruitment process. It is that stage where the best and most qualified out of the many applicants are chosen and given the job. In some organizations, orientation, and training are part of the hiring and onboarding process. During the orientation and training, newly recruited personnel are taken through the rudiments of their jobs, the ideals, values, norms, vision, and mission of the organization, and the organization's expectations of them.

Sources of Recruitment (External and Internal Recruitment)

Two basic ways through which vacancies can be filled in an organization exit. They are the internal and external sources of recruitment.

Internal Sources of Recruitment

Most often, there are qualified personnel in an organization who can fill vacant positions when the need be. For instance, the deputy director for finance and administration can squarely fit into the position of director of finance when the position becomes vacant. If not for anything, the office of the deputy is to support and understudy the office of the substantive director. Also, a director of, for instance, logistics can equally fill the position of director of administration is the position becomes vacant. Finding and hiring qualified employees from within the staff pool of an organization to fill vacant positions in the said organization is referred to as internal recruitment. It can be promotion through intra-departmental recruitment or transfer.

One of the most important ways of filling vacant spaces in an organization is through recruiting internal staff. Filling spaces in the office with internal staff can be done through promotions, transfers, or internships. Promotion denotes the situation where a subordinate or a junior staff is elevated to manage a higher position or rank. Transfers are done when a qualified member of an organization is relocated from their current offices to new places for specific reasons. In some instances, non-permanent staff, such as interns, are given permanent job opportunities if their working ethics are satisfactory to the leaders of an organization. In several instances, apprentices who are qualified and have mastery of their craft are recruited to manage (with supervision) new branches of organizations.

One advantage of an internal source of recruitment is that it reduces the utilization of organizational resources. Resource for orientation, training, and other incentives are normally less with internal recruitments because the personnel is not new, and already in the pool of personnel. Internal recruitment also reduces the time rate used for training on the job. Internal staff seamlessly adapt to an organization's mission and vision at any level because they have been in the organization for some time.

However, such workers can also play a role in collapsing the firm because they know all the avenues of the firm.

External Sources of Recruitment

An external source of recruitment denotes finding and hiring qualified employees from outside the internal staff pool of an organization to fill vacant positions in the said organization. Recruiting outside of the pool of staff in an organization takes time and resources. Methods for recruiting from external sources include accessing talent pools, rehiring former employees, employee exchanges, referrals, previous applicants, interns, and apprentices, attending recruitment events, partnering with agencies, and campus recruitment. One advantage of selecting employees from external sources is that it ignites the staff. Fresh personnel joining a team adds some vigor to the team. It even serves as a sort of competition, which can influence internal employees to work harder. A disadvantage of external recruitment, however, is that it can derail the enthusiasm of current employees, especially those who could have filled the position perfectly. It also wastes an organization's resources and time in training and orientating the new employee.

Finding Job Seekers

Recruiters and human resource officers have ways of reaching job seekers. Although there are several methods, these are the most effective ways to reach job seekers. Human resource practitioners, writers, researchers, and consultants have come out with various ways of reaching prospective employees. While some are general routines, others are job specifics. Some of the ways of recruitment into an organization involve some or all of the following: word of mouth, employee referrals, job and recruitment fairs, internal staff (promotions, transfers, and internships), advertisements, former employees, previous applicants, and recruitment agencies.

Word of Mouth

Some organizations inform their workers to inform people in their circles of a job opportunity in their organization. This is normally done by word of mouth. Workers belong to communities, such as religious groups, ideological groups, classmate or school-year groups, age groups, and several other societies of which some of their members might be searching for employment opportunities. Organizations, therefore, make good use of their workers as advertising agents to broadcast and help fill vacant positions. This approach usually goes with the employee referral approach. After staff members are told to search for possible employees to fill vacant spaces, they are also encouraged to refer job seekers to their organization. This approach is simple, straightforward, and has its target audience already. It saves time and advertising costs for the organization. However, as usual with human nature, current employees might bring in their family or friends who might not be qualified enough for such vacant positions.

Employee Referrals

One of the oldest, most common, and most effective ways of recruiting job seekers is the employee referral approach. This approach allows existing employees to refer or recommend job seekers to their organization for recruitment. Thus, organizations hire new employees through referrals from existing employees. In many situations, existing employees who refer new ones are given incentives. This is to influence other existing workers to refer their colleagues at home, church, or classmates to the organization. In some instances, when a referred worker proves worthy, the existing employee who did the referral gets a promotion in addition to the incentives given just by referring someone to the organization. The advantage of employee referrals is that they inspire existing employees to be unofficial members of the employee search team. The referred candidate gets the job; the employee who referred them gets a reward or bonus. The referral way of reaching job seekers is also very cost-effective. It allows organizations to secure the services of professionals and the best hands/minds without spending much on the search. Another advantage of the employee referral approach to recruitment is that it builds trust. Some studies poved that managers who recruit employees through referral systems tend to trust the new hires because of who recommended them to the organization. They believe that existing workers may not consciously refer lazy, stealing, or wayward personnel to their organization, especially to embarrass the referrer in the end. Employee referral also boosts an organization's pedigree to job seekers because the referral came from a trusted source. One disadvantage of the referral system, it might influence existing employees to refer their family or friends who are not qualified but have been unemployed for some time. Again, familiar faces around a specific task normally drag the job because workers might be tempted to converse more and lose concentration.

Job and Recruitment Fairs

Modern businesses and organizations rely on recruitment events and job fairs to recruit new staff. Job fairs are time-bound programs with the aim of bringing organizations searching for workers and prospective job seekers together in the bid to give employment and get employment, respectively. Job fairs are mostly done with walk-in interviews organized by organizations. This has become possible because, firstly, some organizations, especially small and medium-scale companies, do not have a well-grounded human resource or professional recruitment office or manager to manage the recruitment process. Such companies can only make good use of job and recruitment fairs to fill their vacant positions in the office.

Secondly, though some offices have competent human resources or hiring officers, they see the cost involved in recruiting new staff as expensive and the whole process as cumbersome. Such organizations resort to job and recruitment fairs to recruit. Using recruitment fairs to fill vacant positions in organizations save the organization's resources. It also saves them time and energy. Furthermore, organizations get the opportunity to build a database for their prospective candidates for future employment. It also gives job seekers the opportunity to choose from several options at the same time, which is normally not the case. Job fares give instantaneous jobs to prospective job seekers, too. However, such processes may lead to recruiting unqualified employees since it does not thoroughly exhaust the recruitment process.

Advertisement

Advertisement is one of the oldest and surest ways used by corporate organizations to reach prospective job seekers. Advertisements come in several forms and through several mediums. Before the advent of the internet, the popular form of advertisement was conventionally done through posting bills and posters on walls along popular and busy streets and through traditional media (television, radio, and tabloids). Organizations highly use these traditional sources of information to the public to advertise their products and vacancies at a cost. In fact, some writers argue that these forms of mediums through which firms advertise vacancies have many challenges. To the critics, these mediums did not have the feedback system to know how the advertisement fared until the day of the interview or until the organization started receiving job application letters. They also argue that such mediums delay in advertising wares and vacancies and are even limited in terms of reach and mileage. However, other schools of thought state that these mediums of advertising vacancies have been very effective from time to time, even currently. Some writers assert that posting job posters on walls along principal and busy streets in communities is still one of the most used strategies for reaching job seekers. The introduction of the internet, with its accompanying websites and, currently, social media, has expanded the reach of organizations in advertising job placements. Most companies across the globe have their own websites and social media pages, with the additional advantage of online communities, where information on the company can easily be accessed. Such organizations use the same platforms to advertise possible vacancies. The advantage of the internet and its added platforms is that, unlike traditional media platforms, it gives wide coverage on planetary terms. The internet is accessible from any part of the world simultaneously. It is estimated that over 3.6 billion people worldwide use social media platforms. This gives job placement adverts a bigger worldwide platform and attracts people of different races, qualifications, and orientations. Hence, a job post can potentially reach millions of prospective job seekers in real-time. Another advantage of using the internet is that an organization can target the job post to ensure that only the most relevant candidates apply. Using the internet requires users to sign in using their personal details. This helps to identify people easily. Filling job forms on the Internet also requires other important job information, such as salary range and other conditions of service. This helps to list the required qualifications and experience in such job posts so that only candidates who qualify can apply. The disadvantages of the internet are fake news and the upsurge of scammers. Anyone else can create a site and use it to scam unsuspecting job seekers.

Former Employees

Organizations sometimes look back at the satisfactory performance of past employees and recall them to fill vacant places. Retired employees, for instance, who performed incredibly well when they were active staff, are normally invited by their organizations to hold one position or the other. High-performing and talented past employees who are normally recalled to work in their former organization include retirees, those on study leave, and those who resigned or are on a break due to personal reasons. Organizations know their skills and performance already and believe in their potential. Employing such past employees in an organization does not scare managers as much as recruiting fresh employees. The advantage of employing past employees is that there is trust between the two parties based on past experiences. In such instances, recruitment also takes less time compared to recruiting fresh job seekers. The disadvantage here is that a disgruntled past employee might come back to vindicate past actions meted out to them when they were in the organization. In addition, past employees normally know the loopholes and windows in the organization, and might use it to their advantage.

Previous Applicants

Organizations, conventionally, have data on former applicants. Such organizations reach job seekers by calling on past applicants to ask if they are still interested in the sample, similar or other job placement opportunities available in the organization. Occasionally, most big organizations do this. This approach is meritorious to the organization because it makes searching for prospective job seekers very easy, less time-consuming, and with lesser use of organizational resources. Notwithstanding the positives, organizations can lose talented job seekers through the data system. A job seeker does not wait to be called from the waiting list. They move all the time.

Recruitment Agencies

The recruitment process is actually a cumbersome one. Smaller companies struggle to go through it. As a result, many small and medium-sized businesses without a dedicated HR department or recruitment team turn to staffing agencies and recruitment firms to meet their hiring needs. The recruitment agencies look for the right talent, shortlist relevant candidates, arrange interviews, and finally select the right candidate for the client organization. Recruitment agencies either charge a fixed price for their task or charge a commission for every successful candidate they recruit for an organization. Currently, some even work on a per-minute or per-hour basis and are paid based on the number of hours they spend on any segment of the recruitment process. Recruitment agencies bridge the gap between job-givers and job-seekers. They make it stress-free for job owners and/or managers to reach prospective job seekers and vice versa. Recruitment agencies, however, are in several instances accused of cheating personnel they helped to get jobs. Some are alleged to have halved the salaries of their clients.

Challenges Associated with Recruitment

Recruitment has its own challenges. The challenges are general and particular in nature. Thus, though recruitment in the United States of America might have its own challenges different from the challenges recruitment processes in Africa face, there are general underlying challenges faced by the majority of recruitment processes the world over. The following are some of the challenges associated with recruitment.

Attracting the Right Applicants

One of the basic challenges facing recruitment the world over is the challenge of attracting and getting the right applicants for the vacancies available. Sometimes, a search team might not get the best-fit applicant for the job but might be forced to choose the best among the applicants to fill a vacant position. Attracting a suitable applicant typically relies on the conditions of service associated with the advertised vacancy. If the conditions of service of an advertised position are juicy, many suitable applicants will go for it. Same way top hierarchy positions in organizations attract suitable and best-fit applicants. It is different in the case of a menial job, a low position in an office, and/or poor conditions of service. Few applicants will apply for such jobs with such positions and conditions of service. If a vacancy advert does not attract suitable applicants, recruitment teams are forced to recruit the best fit in the available applicants, who might not be of any class.

Meeting Recruitment Deadlines

Hiring teams aim to recruit swiftly, as vacancies can drain organizational resources, disrupt operations, and impact productivity. Consequently, recruitment or HR departments typically work within set timelines to fill open positions. Though the timeline for recruitment differs from organization to organization depending on the vacancy to fill, it is advisable to make it quickly. No matter how quickly hiring teams would love to recruit, recruitment sometimes drags due to factors beyond the control of the hiring team.

Factors such as unavailability of best-fit candidates in the applicants, scarce resources to aid the hiring team in doing their work efficiently and effectively, inability of hiring teams to reach consensus, and interference by management, among others, may hinder the recruitment process and keep recruitment sagging.

Observing the Impartial Recruitment Process

Recruiting based on meritocracy is very challenging in human institutions. Human institutions are laced with several biases, which may hinder the smooth operations of such organizations and thus hinder the successful hiring of an applicant for a vacant position. Same with the recruitment process; biases, such as nepotism, fear, or favor, and power influence can mar the process. Such actions cloud the smooth operations of the recruitment team and might lead to hiring the wrong applicant.

Impartial recruitment also means following the laid down recruitment procedures and processes to the letter. This is very challenging to observe due to the peculiarity of some recruitment processes.

Ensuring Efficient Recruitment Process

Human resource departments and hiring teams are tasked to recruit the best-qualified applicants to fill vacant positions in organizations. However, sometimes, the human resource department, hiring team, or even the recruitment agency tasked to hire prospective job seekers may be fraught with several challenges during the recruitment process. During the recruitment process, maintaining effective communication, thorough evaluation, seamless coordination, and strict adherence to recruitment principles can sometimes be challenging. The hiring team may delay in communicating essential information to both the applicants and the organization, delay in evaluating the results of applicants, fail to coordinate interview times, or might use their own principles to recruit applicants instead of the laid down principles and procedures.

Getting Data on Job Seekers

One of the most challenging phenomena facing human institutions is the availability of data. Information on most occurrences is either scarce, not up-to-date, or unavailable at all. For a recruitment department to recruit the right applicants, there should be enough current information on the candidates. However, most countries do not have a current and standard pool of data on job seekers, their skills and expertise, and requirements in the world of work.

How to Overcome the Challenges Associated with Recruitment

Though recruitment challenges are eminent in organizations, there are possible ways organizations and/or their recruitment teams can avert these challenges to the barest minimum. The following are some of the ways that the challenges associated with recruitment can be solved.

Clarity of Requirements

Hiring or recruitment teams should be clear about who can perfectly fit the vacant space created in the office. The team should be clear about the skills and expertise required to fill the vacancy declared. Teams should, therefore, give concise description of the requirements the prospective employee needs to have and the role they will play when recruitment.

Meeting Deadlines

It is possible that recruitment teams might miss deadlines. However, recruitment teams can observe some guidelines that might help avert such challenges.

Firstly, the recruitment team can streamline the process by combining certain stages where possible. For instance, they could conduct interviews and review results on the same day, ideally at the interview location. The recruitment team can also communicate back to applicants quickly so that the other processes can follow. Simple recruitment metrics can help aid in this instance.

In addition, the team should prepare a good and realistic interview plan with achievable timelines that can be met, all things being equal. Sometimes, recruitment teams can set long timelines if they feel that short timelines might be challenging to achieve.

Observing the Impartial Recruitment Process

Recruitment teams can follow some principles that can wean them from the human biases that occur in the recruitment process. Recruitment teams can implement structured interviews, use software to guide the interview process, instantly submit applicant scores to a central system, and adhere to strict guidelines governing the recruitment process. Recruitment teams can also set up blind recruitment software that can help conceal the identity of applicants from individual recruitment team members.

Ensuring Efficient Recruitment Process

Recruitment teams must ensure an efficient recruitment process in order to overcome some challenges. Recruitment firms need to efficiently and effectively communicate, evaluate, coordinate, and adhere to the principles of recruitment. Recruitment firms can use recruitment data and recruitment metrics to improve their recruiting process and make more informed decisions.

Building a Strong Hiring Team

Human resource departments, hiring teams, or recruitment agencies must be strong, efficient, and effective enough to help hire right candidates for their respective organizations. In some instances, audit firms have identified unqualified personnel in human resource departments, hiring teams, or recruitment agencies.

Conclusion

Chapter One has been an introductory chapter of what recruitment actually is. The chapter expanded the scope of recruitment beyond just the definition of the concept. It included modern procedures added to the recruitment process, such as orientation and/or initial training of newly appointed applications into an organization.

There are processes involved in recruitment applicants into an organization. Although exit processes may vary by organization, area, zone, or continent, some basic procedures are consistent across all regions. These stages in the dominant process were discussed in the chapter with examples.

The sources of recruitment as to where best-fit employees are found to fill vacancies in organizations were also discussed. The two basic sources, internal and external, were thoroughly discussed.

Challenges abound in human institutions, and neglecting them means finding doom for the organization in question. The chapter, therefore, discusses the challenges associated with most recruitment processes and proffers possible solutions to them.

In conclusion, Chapter One has opened the discussion into the world of recruitment, and the subsequent chapters are going to delve into the other departments of recruitment, with Chapter Two starting with recruitment policy.

Chapter 2:
Recruitment Policy

What Is a Policy?

A policy denotes laid down rules and regulations used to regulate a process or phenomenon. It is also described as a purpose-driven action that deals with an issue of concern. Policy documents involve officially laid down expressions of procedures and stages used in addressing a common issue. A policy involves inputs, outputs, and outcomes.

What Is a Recruitment Policy?

Simply, a recruitment policy details how to hire people. A recruitment policy denotes the rules and regulations guiding the hiring of personnel into organizations. More technically, a recruitment policy is the framework of rules and regulations that outlines all recruitment methods and practices. For a job seeker or applicant to be employed in an organization, the person needs to go through a process that

is sanctioned and guided by a standard recruitment policy. In human resource management, a recruitment policy defines the processes and practices used to attract and hire new talent with the necessary experience, skills, and qualifications to drive the organization's growth and improve its performance.

Modern recruitment policies incorporate past experiences, present conditions and issues, and future prospects of an organization. They also detail the limits that guide the hiring process. Recruitment policies answer the who, what, when, where, and how the recruitment process should be conducted in an organization.

Recruitment policies might differ in size depending on the type of organization. Small and medium firms might choose to have a few pages of guidelines that guide the decisions, actions, and inactions during their recruitment processes. However, big and industrial firms might have bigger documents as their recruitment policy. Large firms might get addendums, sub-policies, and footnotes in their comprehensive recruitment policy documents, but that of smallholder firms might be straightforward. However, the size of a company's recruitment policy document doesn't matter nor decide the success of the firm, but the component of the document.

Features of a Recruitment Policy

Though not constant or static, recruitment policies have some basic features that make it easy to identify them as such. The basic features of a company's recruitment may include some or all of the following:

Policy Statement (Heading and Philosophy)

The philosophy of an organization plays a major role in designing the policies for recruitment. In the end, the prospective employee comes on board to help increase output and make the organization grow. It is, therefore, prudent to draft a recruitment policy for an organization with a clear notion of what the organization's philosophy is and the goals they have.

The heading and philosophy part is the introduction of the policy. This part includes the policy statement that details the general overview of the recruitment policy and what it seeks to achieve. The introduction of a policy statement may read as follows: The organization seeks a fair and transparent recruitment process that is open for all job applicants without discrimination or influence of any kind.

Policy Purpose

The purpose of the recruitment policy document denotes the strategic direction on how to attract and recruit prospective job applicants to help enhance output, meet organizational goals, and boost the growth of the organization. The purpose also clarifies how the attraction and recruitment of applicants should align with international best practices in recruitment rules and regulations.

Policy Standards

An organization's standards are very dear to the leadership and staff. Standards make organizations look credible or otherwise in the eyes of customers. High standards help organizations to maintain consistency

during the recruitment process. Standards must be applied to themes such as equality and fairness in recruiting prospective employees, diversity in the process or style of recruiting staff, and legal requirements attached to the recruitment of staff into an organization. Some authors refer to the recruitment standards as principles. Some of the principles found in recruitment policy include the following.

1. Respect

Recruitment policies express how job applicants should be handled. Most recruitment policy documents state that job applicants must be respected and handled decently. This principle makes applicants also reciprocate the respect given to them, and that breeds sanity in the recruitment process.

2. Integrity

The recruitment policy addresses how the recruitment process should be handled. The recruitment process should be handled in a situation that will make the decisions and actions taken by the recruitment team have the ability to stand the test of time or external review.

3. Transparency

Every step of the recruitment process must be taken transparently. The openness of the recruitment process to all recruitment members, job applicants, and the outside world gives the recruitment process credibility.

4. Fairness

Impartiality and objectivity should be applied by the recruitment team at all levels of the recruitment process. This makes the applicants accept the outcome of the process and have trust in it.

5. Equity

All job-seeking applicants must be treated equally without biases, such as gender, religion, race, tribe, sect, or origin. Treating applicants equitably gives credibility to the recruitment process.

6. Merit

The selected job applicant is selected based on merit, including qualities such as competence, skill, expertise, and/or long service. Giving appointment opportunities based on merit makes other applicants go back and work hard so that they can be selected during the next selection process.

7. Accountability

Recruitment teams should be held responsible and accountable for the outcome of the process. From recruitment planning to selection and onboarding, the recruitment team should be accountable for each stage of the process. Finally, if a not-too good (not the best) applicant is selected, the recruitment team should be responsible for that, and vice versa.

8. Documentation

The recruitment team should document every decision or action taken and justify why that particular decision or action was taken. The team should be able to produce the minutes of every meeting they held in the selection process, from the start to the end. This will help with continuity and referrals in future activities.

Recruitment Procedures

One of the clearly cut features of an organization's recruitment policy is the procedures the recruitment team or human resource department adheres to during recruitment. It helps recruitment teams to select the best fit candidate for an organization. The procedures of a recruitment policy make up the larger part of the whole policy document. Organizations may modify the tenets of recruitment policy procedures to suit their individual preferences and/or targets. Such reformations may touch on the role, skill, and expertise required for declaring such vacant positions.

Procedures of a regular recruitment policy have its basic features, including the following:

1. Prehiring Methods

All the plans, decisions, and actions that are observed before the actual hiring of an employee is done are part of the procedures of a recruitment policy. Prehiring procedures involve mostly recruitment planning. In making decisions at the preplanning stage in the recruitment procedures, the general values, mission statement, and mission of the organizations should not be overlooked. They serve as the guiding principles during the recruitment process.

2. The Hiring Process

The hiring process is essential in every organization's recruitment policy and clearly details how prospective employees should be hired into an organization in question. Though individual companies might have differing procedures as to how to hire a prospective employee, most organizations have similar procedures. Also, the hiring process may be reformed due to factors such as the responsibility of the prospective employee, the attitude of the applicants, natural occurrences, and issues affecting the recruitment team, among others.

3. Hiring Tools

Every recruitment team has tools that aid them in the recruitment process. Recruitment tools, though with room for additions and omissions, are clearly spelled in the organization's recruitment procures that are found in the organization's policy. Organizations take a stand on issues such as the mode of interviewing job applicants, communication, and the style of the interview in their recruitment policy before actual recruitment comes on.

The recruitment procedure has several steps, including vacancy authorization, job description development, and revision, designing selection criteria, vacancy advertisement, the vacancy shortlisting applicants, identification and selection of interview panel, interview assessment tests, and selection of the most suitable applicant for the vacant position in the organization.

Notwithstanding the observance of all these stages in the recruitment process, there should be a police check by the organization before it finally gives an appointment letter to the best-fit applicant. This is to verify that the successful applicant has no criminal record. Additionally, some organizations contact the applicant's previous employer to conduct a reference check. This helps the organization to see how, for example, the successful candidate meets targets, conduct themselves, work under pressure, or meet deadlines.

1 • **Authorization Vacancy**

2 • **Job Description Development**

3 • **Selection Criteria Design**

4 • **Vacancy Announcement and Advertisement**

5 • **Screening and Shortlisting**

6 • **Interview Panel Identification and Selection**

7 • **Assessment and Interview**

8 • **Select Best-Fit Applicant**

Recruitment Procedures Responsibilities

The recruitment policy has a section on responsibility. This section outlines the specific tasks, timelines, and methods for each step. It highlights the responsibilities of each member of the recruitment team, covering their roles from start to finish. In this section, details of who should be in charge of the administration and implementation of the recruitment policy.

For instance, a recruitment policy document shall detail the tasks of the human resource manager, line manager, screening team, interview panel, and even that of the applicants during a recruitment process. While human resource managers, for instance, oversee the entire recruitment process, and the line manager makes recruitment requisitions and takes part in interviews, job-seeking applicants have the responsibility to follow the standards or rules of the recruitment process.

Definitions

Definitions in recruitment policy are the explanations given to specific and technical terms in the policy. Definitions clarify the technical terms in the recruitment policy document and make them accessible to every reader.

References

Policy documents have related documents or other documents from which relevant sections were picked. Such documents are referenced in the recruitment policy document. References show the documents or materials that were referred to or some parts being used while writing the particular policy document.

Review Procedures

Review procedures in recruitment policy documents detail how the policy document can be revised to suit current or changing trends. It details the processes, steps, and ways that a recruitment policy document can be revised when the need be.

Importance of Recruitment Policy

Recruitment policies in organizations guide the recruitment process and help recruit the best-fit job applicant for an organization. The following are some of the reasons why it is necessary to have a recruitment policy in an organization.

Compliance

The presence of a recruitment policy in an organization makes it possible for Human Resource Departments, hiring departments, or recruitment firms tasked by organizations to hire job seekers to follow certain principles and processes. When absent, members of recruitment firms or hiring teams might go wayward in doing what they feel is proper. The presence of a policy guides individuals and teams in recruitment boards to know what to do, how to do it, when to do it, and where to do it. International recruitment policy has made people abide by similar rules, regulations, and processes in hiring persons into organizations.

It also enhances the adherence to labour laws in a country. Every state has its labor laws. The recruitment policy of organizations helps the organizations to work in line with the labor laws of the countries such organizations are situated.

Similarly, recruitment policy also contains how to fire nonperforming or con-complying workers. Thus, acts that could make an employee lose their job in one organization can make another lose their job in another organization.

Enhances Transparency

Using a recruitment policy in the process of recruiting new applicants guarantees transparency and respect for the process. It allows everybody to be in the known of what is actually happening during the recruitment process. It also makes job applicants who could not secure the job position even accept that the one chosen was better than them due to the transparency of the process.

Enhances Credibility

Recruitment that is done in line with the tenets of a recruitment policy gives credibility to the recruitment process and bestows some respect to the recruited job applicant. Complying with recruitment policy when recruiting new personnel for an organization protects organizations from the legal responsibility that emanates when other applicants feel unfairly treated or discriminated against by the recruitment team.

Enhances the Probability of Choosing the Right Person

When recruiting departments or firms go by the tenets of recruitment policies during the recruiting process, it enhances the chances of hiring the best-fit job seeker for the vacancy declared. Recruitment policies are thoroughly thought out and a well-schemed set of rules and procedures put up by industry players with great experience, skills, expertise, and adequate knowledge in the field of recruitment. Using policies compiled by such great minds guarantees a higher probability of selecting the right candidate at the end of the process.

Uniformity and Consistency

The presence of a recruitment policy in an organization enhances constancy. It makes the recruitment process the same or similar, with fewer changes in other organizations. In effect, what is applicable in one region is applicable in other regions, with slight differences in the application of the tenets of the policy.

The recruitment policy has unique uniformity and consistency. Globally, there are basic uniform rules and codes that guide recruitment policies in every organization. Although there might be slight changes in the recruitment policies of individual organizations to suit local or individual interests, most standard recruitment policies are similar. In effect, there is common compliance and application of procedures and rules in every organization across the globe.

Despite the uniformity and consistency in adhering to recruitment policy principles, some human resource departments or recruitment agencies may sometimes exceed or deviate from the fundamental standards of international recruitment policies. Recruitment agencies are human institutions, and they bend the rules anytime they feel uneasy with the application of such policies.

Challenges Associated with Recruitment Policy

Policies, just like every human venture, have their challenges. Modern policies on recruitment have their own general and peculiar challenges affecting them. Some of the challenges include the following:

Adoption and Adaptation

Recruitment policies are laid down rules that are supposed to regulate the process of hiring new employees into organizations. It is one thing to know the rules and another thing to adopt and adapt to the tenets of recruitment policies. Some of the tenets of a particular recruitment policy can become very challenging to adapt to due to it being too technical or due to internal or external issues, such as leadership style in the organization, availability of resources, and the time frame allotted to the recruited process, among others.

In addition, some review procedures are hard to meet. Some are technically inclined to specific areas, positions, or even departments that make it difficult to suit local style. Others are out of reach, no matter how the recruitment team manipulates it. It is, therefore, challenging for recruitment to follow the tenets of a particular recruitment policy to the letter.

Implementation

The implementation of policies makes it complete. In some instances, implementing a policy becomes problematic due to particular articles or tenets they have in them. For example, a policy requiring applicants to hold a postgraduate degree may be difficult to enforce if, during the screening stage, it is discovered that none of the applicants possess this qualification. It is arguable though, but most policies cannot be implemented to the core. There might be a particular instance where the implementation team (recruitment team) sees some part of the policy as unattainable.

Lifespan of Policy

Policies have a lifespan of relevance. Beyond that stage, the relevance and efficacy of the policy wanes. This may be due to factors such as time, modernity, transformations of the organizational structure, or even the expansion or otherwise of the organization.

When policies stay the same for a longer period without reforms to meet the modern or changing needs of the business or organizational structure, they lose efficacy. For instance, a fifty-year-old policy that expressed that the recruitment team should only use one-on-one interviews to select the best applicant has become mundane and inefficacious currently due to the inception of telephone and online interviews, such as Zoom conferencing.

Resource Availability

Policy implementation goes with the availability of resources, both human and material. Some recruitment policies might be challenging to implement due to the unavailability of or limited resources available to help implement them. For example, a company with limited resources might find it difficult to execute a policy tenet that states that the organization should do a series of interviews before it chooses a suitable applicant.

Sample Recruitment Policy 1

This Employee Recruitment and Selection Policy template is ready to be tailored to your company's needs and should be considered a starting point for setting up your recruiting policies.

Policy Brief and Purpose

Our employee recruitment and selection policy describes our process for attracting and selecting external job candidates. This recruitment policy sample can serve as a rubric that our recruiters and hiring managers can use to create an effective hiring process.

We are committed to our equal opportunity policy at every selection stage. Hiring teams should aim for a well-planned and discrimination-free hiring process.

Scope

This recruitment and selection policy applies to all employees who are involved in hiring for our company. It refers to all potential job candidates.

Policy Elements

What is the recruitment and selection process?

Generally, hiring teams could go through the following steps:

☒ Identify the need for an opening

☒ Decide whether to hire externally or internally

☒ Review the job description and compose a job ad

☒ Select appropriate sources (external or internal) for posting the opening

☒ Decide on the selection stages and possible timeframe

☒ Review résumés in company database/ATS

☒ Source passive candidates

☒ Shortlist applications

☒ Proceed through all selection stages

☒ Run background checks

☒ Select the most suitable candidate

☒ Make an official offer

Stages may overlap. Hiring managers may remove/add steps as appropriate. The first five stages are mandatory in every hiring process.

Posting Jobs Internally

Hiring managers can post a job opening internally before starting to recruit external candidates. If they decide to post internally, they can:

☒ Set a deadline for internal applications

☒ Communicate their opening through newsletters, emails, word of mouth, or an Applicant Tracking System's automated email.

Creating Job Descriptions

Hiring managers can create job ads based on full job descriptions of each role. Job ads should be clear and accurately represent the open position. They should include the following:

☒ A brief description of our company and mission

☒ A short summary of the role's purpose

☒ A list of responsibilities

☒ A list of requirements

☒ How to apply

The job ad's style should be consistent with our company's unique voice. It should be addressed to you in a polite and engaging tone.

Jargon, complicated phrases, and gender-specific language should be avoided.

Employee Selection Stages

Our company has a standard hiring process that may be tweaked according to a role's requirements. Our standard process involves the following:

☒ Résumé screening

☒ Phone screening

☒ Assignment

☒ Interview

Hiring managers may choose to add/remove stages depending on the role they're hiring for. For example, they can add the following selection stages/methods:

☒ Assessment centers

☒ Group interviews

☒ Competency/Knowledge or other selection tests

☒ Referrals' evaluation

In most cases, the stages of résumé screening and interview are compulsory.

Interview Feedback

Recruiters/hiring managers should always inform candidates they interviewed that they decided to reject them. Leaving candidates in the dark can be damaging to our employer's brand.

Also, we encourage hiring managers to send interview feedback to candidates. They should first, though, check with HR to make sure they won't invite legal action. Being brief, respectful, and keeping feedback job-related are the general rules for writing feedback emails to candidates.

Revoked Offers

In case a formal has to be revoked, the hiring manager and the human resources department should draft and sign an official document. This document should include a legitimate reason for revoking the offer. Legitimate reasons include the following:

☒ The candidate is proven not to be legally allowed to work for our company at a specific location

☒ Candidate has falsified references or otherwise lied about a serious issue ☒ Candidate doesn't accept the offer within the specified deadline (deadline must have been included in the offer letter)

Hiring managers and HR must notify the candidate formally as soon as possible.

Disclaimer: This policy template is meant to provide general guidelines and should be used as a reference. It may not consider all applicable local, state, or federal laws and is not a legal document. Neither the author nor Workable will assume any legal liability that may arise from the use of this policy.

Sample Recruitment Policy 2

This is an excerpt of the Recruitment Policy in the National Conditions of Service Policy for Staff of the Local Government Service of Ghana.

2.1.4. Creation of a Department

Proposals for the creation of a new department shall be submitted by the Regional Coordinating Council (RCC) and Metropolitan, Municipal, and District Assemblies (MMDA) to the Local Government Service Council for consideration and approval.

The proposals shall specify the following:

a) Proposed name of the new department

b) Justification for creating the new department

c) Objectives and functions of the department

d) Number of departmental and general posts that may be created and grouped into the new department

e) Scheme of Service of the new Department.

2.1.5. Creation of Posts

a) The creation of all local government service posts shall be approved by the Local Government Service Council, which shall be the authority in this matter.

b) Applications for the creation of any post shall be submitted by the appropriate organization (LGSS, Regional Coordinating Council / Metropolitan, Municipal, and District Assembly) to the Local Government Service Council. The application shall indicate the following:

i. The title of the post to be created

ii. The justification for creating the post

iii. The total complement of staff required

iv. Statement of duties and qualifications

v. Salary scale

vi. Scheme of service (for new post)

c) The Local Government Service Council, in conveying approval, shall state the following:

i. The title of the new post

ii. The salary level

iii. The qualifications

iv. Progression and the complement of posts

v. Whether the new posts are general or departmental

2.1.6. Departmental and Grade Transfers

Transfers of officers in the service from one department to another or the transfer of officers from one grade in an occupational group to another may be considered by the relevant appointing authority. Officers wishing to transfer from one grade in an occupational group or department to another may after obtaining the necessary clearance from their head of department or occupational group to which they wish to transfer, submit a request for consideration by the head of service.

2.1.7. Methods of Filling

The mode of filling vacancies shall be by promotion, demotion, and direct appointment through external/internal advertisement, secondment, and transfer into the service.

2.2. Appointment

All appointments in the service shall be by the president on the advice of the Local Government Service Council in consultation with the Public Services Commission.

2.2.1. Category A Posts

The appointing authority for Category A posts in the Local Government Service shall be the president of Ghana, acting on the advice of the Local Government Service Council, given in consultation with the Public Services Commission.

2.2.2. Categories B to F Posts

The appointing authority for Categories B, C, D, E, and F posts shall be the Local Government Service Council in consultation with the Public Service Commission in accordance with the approved scheme of service.

2.3. Conditions for Appointment

Appointments into the Local Government Service shall be subject to a candidate satisfying the conditions specified for entry into the grade. Candidates must be declared medically fit by a medical officer from a government hospital. Unless otherwise specified, all appointments within the service will be full-time, and the appointees will hold substantive positions. Any activities outside the scope of the appointment carrying additional remuneration can only be accepted or undertaken with the permission of the council.

2.3.1. Effective Date of Appointment

The effective date of appointment upon entry into the service shall be the date on which the officer reports for duty.

2.3.2. Acceptance of Appointment

Acceptance of a fresh appointment shall be notified not later than the stated deadline in the appointment letter. After the stipulated period, the appointment shall be deemed to have lapsed and the appointing authority shall reserve the right to offer the appointment to another candidate.

2.3.3. Appointment of Convicted Persons

Convicted persons, other than those convicted on grounds of dishonesty, homicide, and moral turpitude, may be considered for appointment into the Local Government

Service. Persons convicted of dishonesty, homicide, and moral turpitude may, however, be considered for appointment, subject to the lapse of at least ten years after such conviction or unconditional pardon granted by the president of the Republic of Ghana.

2.3.4. Appointment of Non-Ghanaians

The service may appoint non-Ghanaians on a limited engagement basis when there is no available Ghanaian expertise in the relevant fields. The appointment of non-Ghanaians to the Local Government Service shall comply with the laws of Ghana.

2.4. Acting Appointment/Assignment

Where it becomes imperative to request an officer to perform the functions of a superior officer for a period exceeding three (3) months, an acting appointment shall be conferred on him by the head of the service. The president shall be the appointing authority for acting appointments in respect of the head of the service. Conditions for acting appointments are as follows:

a) No officer shall be appointed to a position that is more than one step above his/her present grade.

b) The officer holding the acting appointment shall be paid the difference between his/her salary and the entry salary point of the grade for which he/ she has been appointed to act.

c) No acting appointment shall exceed a period of one year.

d) An officer who has performed satisfactorily in an acting capacity for more than one year may be considered for promotion to the grade for which he/ she acted.

e) Allowances/benefits attached to the position shall be paid to the officer occupying the acting position.

Acting assignments may be made under the following circumstances:

a) Upon the death of the substantive officer.

b) When the substantive officer resigns, retires, or vacates his/her post.

c) When the substantive officer proceeds on the course, duty overseas, or leaves without pay.

d) When the substantive officer is dismissed, removed, suspended, or interdicted from duty.

2.5. Limited Engagement/Contracts

Retired staff appointed on limited engagement terms shall serve on a monthly or yearly basis, with the option for renewal at the discretion of the appointing authority. For the avoidance of doubt, no retired staff who is sixty-five (65) years old or above shall benefit from this dispensation.

2.6. Appointee's Particulars

Letters of appointment shall specify the following terms of the appointment:

a) Job title

b) Type of appointment (permanent, temporary, contract, etc.) c) Effective date of appointment

d) Probation period (if any)

e) Salary scale and starting point

f) Brief job description

g) Posting instructions (where applicable)

h) Other relevant benefits as contained in the approved Conditions of Service

2.7. Oath of Secrecy/Allegiance

All officers who occupy the position of Director, their analogous grades, and above, shall swear the Oath of Secrecy and allegiance to be administered by the Head of Service and that of the Head of Service to be administered by the Council Chairman.

2.8. Hours of Work

The standard working hours shall be forty (40) hours per week with eight hours a day. The hours of work start from 8:00 a.m. to 5:00 p.m. with a one (1) hour break at 12:30 p.m. Senior staff may be required to work beyond normal working hours if the job requires it. This extra work will not attract overtime allowance.

2.9. Probation

A newly appointed officer of the Local Government Service shall serve a probationary period of six (6) months with effect from the date he/she assumes duty. Where the appointing authority is not satisfied that the conduct and job performance of the officer have been satisfactory, it shall proceed to either terminate the appointment or extend the probationary period by a further period of three (3) months. The probation period is counted as part of the minimum years new entrants shall serve before they are considered for promotion.

2.10. Confirmation

A formal letter of confirmation shall be issued accordingly. Unless informed in writing to the contrary, a newly employed staff who has completed such probationary period shall be deemed to have been confirmed in his/her post.

Conclusion

Recruitment policy, like any other policy, contains the rules and regulations used in regulating processes or phenomena. It gives procedural clues on how things or concepts should be managed from the start to the end. This chapter expressed a policy as the combination of inputs, outputs, and outcomes of a recruitment process.

The chapter discussed the features of a modern recruitment policy, the importance or essence of a modern recruitment policy, and the challenges associated with a modern recruitment policy. A sample recruitment policy has also been shared in this chapter to give a clue about what recruitment policies look like.

Chapter 3:
Recruitment Agencies

What Is a Recruitment Agency?

As expressed in Chapter One, the recruitment process is very arduous. The challenge emanates from the fact that organizations and employment seekers have different needs. It needs professional expertise and great skill to balance the organizational interest and the needs of job seekers. Due to this, most organizations spend a great deal of resources on equipping their human resource departments or recruitment staff. In most organizations, the budget allocated to the human resource department outweighs that for the other departments. Consequently, most organizations prefer to outsource the recruitment function to external organizations with the expertise and personnel to handle their core production responsibility. These are what are referred to as recruitment agencies.

A recruitment agency, therefore, is an organization that specializes in matching employers to prospective job seekers. In short, recruitment agencies link employers and job seekers. Such agencies serve as liaisons for firms looking for people to employ and for people looking for jobs to do. Recruitment agencies look for the right talent, shortlist relevant candidates, arrange interviews, and finally select the right candidate for the organization. Recruitment agencies bridge the gap between job givers and job seekers. They make it stress-free for job owners and/or managers to reach prospective job seekers and vice versa.

The outsourcing of staffing arrangements (recruitment) to external agents is not an emerging trend in the world, especially in countries with a free market system of ideology. There is a growing number of people recruited through externalization the world over, and there has been a surge in the registration of agencies that specialize in recruiting professional, skilled, and casual/seasonal workers in America relative to those recruited via many organizations' internalization process. For example, the Bureau of Labor Statistics in the United States of America reports that employment through the agency system has almost tripled in the last ten years. It is also estimated that nearly 90 percent of the United States of America's businesses recruit their workers through the recruitment agency system.

The reason for this rising trend in recruitment agencies is several. While some authors believe that it emanates from the organizations' strategic reactions to the ever-increasing economic challenges and constant demand for more flexibility from their direct employees, others also assert that it is one way of creating more jobs and expanding the base of the industry. The monthly labor review of the United States of America's Department of Labor (DOL) expresses that the rising level of recruitment agencies is due to their ability to fill short-term job assignments, the flexibility and simplicity in replacing emergency vacancies, and their strong bargaining power for both the employer and the job seeker. Some arguments also posit that it is incomprehensible for an organization's internal recruitment staff or its human resource department to spend time and resources to recruit, especially non-experts, non-skilled, and non-permanent workers, particularly part-time or intermittent workers, such as students, etc.

It is believed that most of the employees recruited into organizations through recruitment agencies are temporary or contingent workers, as is the case in the United States of America and Canada. In most European countries, such employees are referred to as temporary employees, fixed-term employees, or non-permanent employees. In Australia and New Zealand, employees recruited through recruitment agencies are mostly referred to as casual employees. These names given by various countries on various continents informed my decision to borrow Djibo et al. 2010 and Polivka and Nardone's 1989 definition of temporary labor or contingent work as "any job in which an individual does not have an explicit or implicit contract for long-term employment." It is estimated that about 90 percent of employees working in organizations in the United States of America are contingent workers.

An agent is a person or tool used in implementing a specific task. A recruitment agent is a personnel who works in recruitment agencies and facilitates the recruitment process. Recruitment agents make things run in the agency.

Responsibilities of a Recruitment Agency/Agent

As stated earlier in this chapter, the recruitment process is very involving. It, therefore, needs a competent body with the required skills and expertise to search for talents, shortlist relevant candidates out of

the lot that applied for the vacant position arranges interviews for the applicants, scores the applicant's performance during the interview, and finally selects the right candidate for the organization.

A recruitment agency manages the recruitment process on behalf of an organization. The functions of a recruitment agency include the following:

Recruitment Planning

A recruitment agency is responsible for the planning of the recruitment process. Recruitment agencies bring the necessary skills and expertise to manage the technical nature of the recruitment process, ensuring it is handled effectively by qualified personnel. Recruitment agencies discuss and plan the number or type of vacancies to be declared, the job specifications to be assigned to the prospective employee, qualifications and competencies required to fill the vacant post, remuneration, and other conditions of service to be given to the prospective employee, and other modules for the office or portfolio created.

Identifying Human Resource Needs in Organizations

Recruitment agencies assist organizations in identifying the roles and departments that contribute to their growth. Many new businesses rely on recruitment agencies to pinpoint the expertise and skills needed to enhance performance and drive better results. Recruitment agencies look at the vision and mission statement and other ideas of the new setup and create the offices and personnel the firm would need.

Declaring Vacant Position

Recruitment agencies declare vacancies for organizations. Some organizations prefer to remain anonymous when hiring, entrusting recruitment agencies with the responsibility of publicly announcing their job openings. Such announcements usually start with sentences such as "a reputable company is looking to employ the services of . . ." without clearly which organization it is that is looking for the employees. Recruitment agencies declare vacant positions after identifying the human resource needs of the organization.

Vacancy declaration and advertisement highlight the following salient points: qualifications, skills, and experience required; the remuneration; terms of the appointment; and core functions of the job.

Finding Prospective Job Seekers

After declaring a position in an office or organization vacant, the process of finding a prospective employee to fill that vacant space starts. Recruitment agencies find prospective people to fill a vacant position through either internal source or external sources. With the internal source of recruitment, the recruitment agency looks within the organization to pick a current employee to fill the vacant position. An external source of recruitment is when the recruitment agency picks a prospective job applicant from outside the working pool of the organization.

Screening and Shortlisting Job Seekers

Screening is the process of sieving the applications for and choosing the qualified applicants for further selection. Screening commences after sourcing of candidates is done. It is the responsibility of recruitment agencies to do screening and shortlisting on behalf of the organization. It is part of the recruitment process. Recruitment agencies review applications, which include cover or application letters, résumés or curriculum vitae, and other attached particulars, such as birth certificates, educational and professional certificates, and National Service Certificates (as pertaining to Ghana and other West African Countries), among others.

Recruitment agencies dig deeper to know why a prospective job seeker left their previous job (if any) or reasons for applying for the current job. They also check the correctness of addresses, referees, arrangement and wording of the curriculum vitae or profile, and expressions during the screening and shortlisting. Shortlisting helps recruitment agencies remove unqualified applications and gives room to deal with few qualified applicants.

Screening and shortlisting involve preparing a list of applications received; screening candidates against their qualifications, experience, and competencies stated in the job description; scoring candidates in order of merit; preparing a report of candidates who meet the shortlisting criteria; and preparing a report of candidates who do not meet the shortlisting criteria.

Interviewing Prospective Job Seekers

Recruitment agencies schedule interview sessions for qualified job applicants after screening and shortlisting. The recruitment agency hired to assist with employee hiring is responsible for scheduling interview dates, times, and locations. In some cases, the agency may assign a team of interviewers to conduct the sessions when contracted by an organization to find candidates. Some recruitment agencies outsource the interview of prospective applicants to interview experts. In the end, it is the best-qualified applicant that the recruitment team wants to hire for the organization that contracted them.

Specific activities that are undertaken during interview sessions include preparation of the interview schedule, invitation of shortlisted applicants for the interview, forming the interview panel, training the interview panel, designing interview questions, and conducting the interview itself.

Reviewing the Performance of Interviewees

The next stage that recruitment firms are tasked to observe in the recruitment process is the reviewing of applicants' performances during the interview session. In some instances, recruitment firms take the raw scores of interviews to professional bodies for review. Recruitment agencies set standards, such as accuracy of response or answers, timing, reasoning power, personality, dress code, confidence level, and posture, during the interview session for scoring and reviewing interview scores. Performance review includes scoring applicants and preparing interview reports.

Hiring and Onboarding Job Seekers

Recruitment firms finally hire and integrate prospective job applicants into the organizations that need human resources. Selecting the best out of applicants needs the input of all the recruitment team members. Most times, it is at this level the organization that is employing gets to know its prospective employees. Successful applicants are introduced to the employing organization. The work of the recruitment agency ends after hiring and onboarding until another contract comes.

Training Employees (In-Service Training)

Recruitment agencies also train employees for organizations. This is known as in-service training. To remain competitive in the evolving work environment, an organization's staff requires ongoing training and retraining on the latest international best practices in their respective fields and departments. Some recruitment agencies have built strong relationships with organizations by specializing in staff training and development. The recruitment agencies broker contracts between organizations and training agencies, or the recruitment agencies themselves might have departments that specialize in training personnel.

Challenges Faced by Recruitment Agencies

Recruitment agencies have peculiar internal and external challenges that affect their existence, operations, and efficacy in delivery. Some of the challenges faced by recruitment firms worldwide include the following.

Challenging Start-Ups

Starting an organization is one of the most difficult tasks in an organizational success. Several people have the skill and expertise to start a firm of any sort. But the resources to start with, especially capital, are very difficult to come by. Most financial and lending institutions do not offer loan opportunities to new business owners. Even when loans are available, securing guarantors can be a significant challenge. Only a few individuals are fortunate enough to receive support from family or friends to help them launch their businesses smoothly. Some are also lucky to get people to help them with space and equipment or even serve as guarantors for start-up loans. It is, therefore, challenging for several new recruitment firms to start.

Struggling to Be Acceptable

It takes time and effort for every organization to be accepted and contacted by clients. Many recruitment firms worldwide are struggling to be recognized even after setting up. Clients do not or are skeptical about giving work to new firms for fear that the firms might not be able to deliver on their responsibilities. In effect, most recruitment firms have been denied great opportunities that could have given them the platform to be internationally accepted and recognized.

Stiff Competition

Competition occurs in every sphere. From human endeavors to the political and business world, competition is imminent. Recruitment agencies face several competitions, internally and externally. Internally, there are several recruitment firms, from mushroom to well-established firms, chasing a few clients and contracts. This creates challenges for businesses, particularly when a company lacks the right contacts. Some organizations choose to rely on their human resource departments for recruitment, regardless of whether the staff there are qualified for this specific task. Also, the cost involved in hiring a recruitment firm to help in the recruitment process makes organizations rely on their human resource personnel. It has, therefore, become an open competition between human resource departments of organizations and recruitment firms when it comes to recruitment.

Insufficient Qualified Personnel

The art of recruitment is a skill people have to master in order to do a job. Sheer education cannot make one a perfect recruitment officer. It takes the requisite education, years of practice, and learning on the job to master. Thus, most recruitment firms are facing challenges with getting the needed personnel to work with. Sometimes, too, skilled practitioners reject working in recruitment agencies since they know that organizations shall contact them personally when there is a vacancy to fill. In the end, recruitment firms are left with fluffy personnel to manage, which clients would also not be pleased to work with.

Unfavorable Government Policy

Government policies in individual countries might not work favorably for organizations, including recruitment organizations. For instance, a harsh taxation system by a government may lead many recruitment agencies to crumble. Most recruitment firms find it difficult to get clients constantly. They, however, need to file their taxes every year. It, therefore, becomes difficult for struggling recruitment firms to pay their taxes yearly and also stay in business. Consequently, most recruitment firms fold up easily. Again, high demands for business registration might make it challenging for new start-ups, including recruitment agencies.

Solving the Challenges Facing Recruitment Agencies

Same way, recruitment agencies face different challenges; same vein, they can solve some of these challenges. The following are ways that recruitment agencies can solve some of the challenges affecting them.

Resource Pull in Building Start-Ups

One of the best ways to start an organization is by pulling resources together. Although challenging, it is possible and practical for like-minded individuals to pool their resources and start a business from the ground up. People can contribute their life savings, take small loans from family and friends, or secure grants from other organizations to collectively fund the venture. In some instances, one might have the space, another might have some equipment, and others can also provide some cash to bankroll the new start-up.

Acceptability

Trying to be accepted is challenging. Firms need to show past jobs to be given new ones. The simplest way firms can be accepted is to start taking contracts pro bono mostly. New start-ups can take contracts to recruit for smaller firms free of charge. Clean-free jobs will give new firms records to show when going for high-profile contracts.

Competition

In a competitive world, individuals or firms need to play smart to stay relevant. Instead of competing with each other, recruiting firms can join hands in taking contracts. Also, human resource departments in organizations can sublet some of the stages in the recruitment process to recruitment firms. Joining hands together by technical people breeds perfection.

Availability of Qualified Personnel

Recruitment agencies can do more in-service training for their workers to build their skill set and expertise. Also, recruitment firms can invite personnel from other firms or two or more firms can join hands to build a strong team that can take any contract of recruiting applicants for organizations.

Favorable Government Policy

State governments can reduce taxes to make room for more start-up firms in countries. Financial commitments by recruitment firms can be lessened so they can stay in business. Governments should implement tax holidays and other incentives that lessen the load of firms to help cushion recruitment firms so they can survive.

Sources of Income to Recruitment Agencies

Recruitment agencies are profit-making bodies. Two basic ways through which recruitment agencies make cash are the following.

Applicants Pay for Services

Most recruitment agencies charge job-seeking applicants a token for searching for employment opportunities for them. Linking employment opportunities to prospective employees gives recruitment agencies some cash that they use to run the firm.

Commission on Client Salary of Allowances

Recruitment agencies also make money from commissions on the allowances and salaries their clients take after helping them get employed. An employee in a cleaning organization expressed that the recruitment agency that helped her secure placement in an organization deducts 7 percent (7%) of her salary every month.

Advantages Associated with Recruitment Agencies

Recruitment firms are trained agencies solely mastered in helping organizations get employees and linking job-seeking applicants to prospective organizations. Recruitment agencies act as intermediaries, connecting organizations with job-seeking applicants. The involvement of recruitment firms in the hiring process offers several advantages to organizations. Some of the advantages associated with recruitment agencies include the following.

Smooth and Fast Hiring Process

The presence of recruitment firms in countries helps organizations to locate job seekers without stress. It also gives prospective employees links to where they can find jobs. Bridging the gap between finding employees by organizations and finding jobs by prospective employees solves one of the basic challenges in the recruitment process. It creates a safe and smooth grounds for the recruitment process to start.

Using a recruitment agency can speed up the time it takes for organizations to find new employees. Recruitment agencies have an immense pool of applicants, their expertise and skills, and their prospective fields already stored in their database. They also have a network of connections comprising organizations, professional bodies, and personnel to leverage. The recruitment firms have access to a complex and wide variety of systems that also help them to locate people with hard-to-find skills. Recruitment agencies have gone through almost all the processes of recruitment, except hiring and onboarding, before putting the name of a candidate into their database. The combination of the The above qualities give recruitment agencies the opportunity to produce a suitable applicant for a vacant position at a faster rate.

This also saves organizations time and resources that they would have used in searching for a candidate.

Reduces Workload of Organizations

The human resource department of an organization is tasked with primarily ensuring the welfare of personnel in the organization and allocating skills and expertise to particular tasks or offices. Hiring officers or departments also specifically help recruit new employees into the organization. Other affiliate responsibilities, however, may hinder the core work of the hiring department in times when the organization needs to recruit a new employee. Recruitment firms come in handy. Recruitment firms stand in for the human resource departments and hiring officers when they have so many tasks to perform at the moment.

Enhances the Recruitment of Quality Candidates

Hiring employees through recruitment agencies enhances the rate of getting high-quality candidates with the appropriate skills and expertise. We have access to a large talent pool of prescreened and referenced candidates. Recruitment agencies already have a talent pool from which they can fish a suitable candidate any time there is a vacancy somewhere. Thus, carefully assessed, interviewed, and accepted candidates are already on a waiting list for selection the moment an organization seeks the services of a recruitment agency in recruiting a new employee. On the other hand, most recruitment agencies are specialized in recruiting particular skills or expertise for certain industries. Because recruitment agencies deal with applicants regularly, they keep details of qualified applicants. Any time the services of those people are needed, they provide them.

Knowledge of the Market

Recruitment agencies are masters in their game. They know every corner, organization, and applicant in the industry. Using recruitment firms in the recruitment process is going in for the best candidate, for they know which candidate best suits which position and for which organization.

Recruitment agencies know and actually determine salary rates. They also know the available skill sets, career prospects, contract support, current hiring complexities, and market trends in the sector. Recruitment agencies, therefore, can provide organizations and job-seeking applicants with valuable and sage advice in recruiting.

Client Prioritization

The primary objective of a recruiting agency is to satisfy its client. The client in this context is both the organization in which there is a vacancy and the job-seeking applicant. The recruitment agency sees to it that the organization gets a suitable applicant to fill a vacant position. The recruitment agency also sees to it that the job-seeking applicant on their talent pool list gets a reputable and well-paying organization to work with. That is the satisfaction the recruitment agency gets before even getting paid.

Recruitment agencies, therefore, serve the interests of both the organization and the (prospective) employee.

Enhances Organizational Growth and Development

Working with recruitment services enhances the growth and development of organizations. A recruitment agency communicates with both employers and job seekers. They help train and talk to employees in organizations who are on their lists. They also work with different organizations in their sector, and they become part of the power brokers. Working with recruitment agencies, therefore, opens more opportunities for both businesses and applicants in the sector.

Disadvantages Associated with Recruitment Agencies

Despite the number of advantages associated with recruitment agencies, they still have some challenges when working with them. The following are some of the disadvantages associated with recruitment agencies around the world.

Relatively Expensive

Relying on recruitment agencies to help recruit applicants to an organization comes with its own cost. Most times, the cost is even higher than using the hiring department of the said organization. In fact, it is believed that using recruitment agencies is an expensive endeavor.

Firstly, recruitment agencies charge fees of between 20 percent to 40 percent of an employee's annual salary when they recruit for an organization. The cost can be unbearable if an organization is looking for an applicant to fill a vacant position or looking for a not-easy-to-fill role. In-house hiring officers will not charge anything for recruitment made for their organization.

Again, recruitment agencies add the cost of interview venue, logistics, transportation, and sometimes, even accommodation to their overall cost, which, in the end, bloats the budget of the recruitment process. In the end, only a few top-notch big brands can hire recruitment agencies for the recruitment process.

No or Less Employer Presence in the Recruitment Process

Using an organization's in-house personnel, such as the human resource office or the organization's hiring department, infuses a certain level of organizational presence in the process. It creates the platform for applicants to personally interact with leaders of the organization they may be working with if successful. It also opens the doors for applicants to have insight into the organization they are going to work with before being employed.

Using recruitment firms on behalf of organizations in the recruitment process is different. There is no or very less organizational presence in the recruitment process when an organization uses a recruitment agency to hire its employees. Since the recruitment agency handles everything and has no personal affiliation with the organization it represents, the organization remains anonymous throughout the recruitment process. Applicants tend to remember their first impressions for a long time. Any action or decision made by the recruitment agency rather affects the brand of the organization later, especially if the action or decision taken is negative.

Using recruitment agencies also makes organizations miss one big opportunity to market itself to applicants, some of whom would not make it to the interview session. Recruitment firms rather put their banners, pull-ups, and posters at recruitment centers. This feat markets the recruitment agency, which is paid for its services.

Scandal-Filled Agencies

Getting genuine recruitment agencies to deal with currently is becoming increasingly challenging. Most agencies have tainted their brand with one scandal or another. The profit-motive mindset of modern recruitment agencies is making most of them lurk in schemes that end up being scams. In fact, there are instances where some people have masterminded grand schemes to scam people through recruitment processes.

In addition, there have been several recorded scenarios of mushroom agencies and hard-to-locate agencies. Some agencies sprung up due to a particular recruitment process that was pending. They collapse immediately after they finish the contract or do not get it at all. Other agencies do not even have permanent addresses, landmarked locations, or officially registered licenses to operate. Dealing with an agency with any of these characters is very difficult and may mostly end in a scam.

Other corrupt acts, such as bribery and nepotism, also make recruitment agencies lose their credibility in the selection process. Many recruitment agencies face criticism for selecting applicants based on their ability to pay or through personal connections, even if they are not the most qualified for the role. In some cases, agencies choose which candidates to recommend for positions without considering the specific qualifications or requirements. These practices undermine the integrity of the recruitment process.

Undue Attachment to Organizations

Recruitment agencies have huge biases tilted toward the organization they work or work for. The profit-making motive makes recruitment agencies pay more attention and attract to the recruiting organization and neglect the applicant. In the end, the applicant gets cheated when they are finally employed. Most recruitment agencies do not mind teaming with the organization they are working for to cheat employees. There are numerous ongoing court cases across various continents involving recruitment agencies that have colluded with organizations to deceive employees out of their money. Because recruitment agencies are paid by their client (organizations or employers), most of them can be quite indifferent to the plight or welfare of the employees recruited through them.

Less Cultural Fit

Recruitment agencies help organizations to recruit applicants. Recruitment agencies are well-equipped to help organizations find candidates with the right qualifications and expertise. However, they cannot guarantee a cultural fit for their recommended applicants. This is because few recruitment agencies are familiar with the organizational culture of the companies they recruit for, as well as the backgrounds of the applicants. Agencies may, therefore, recruit a candidate who does not fit into the culture of the organization they helped recruit into.

Apathetic to Applicants

Recruitment agencies are mostly apathetic to the plight of applicants. This is so because they are mostly inclined to the employer or the organization they recruit for. Agencies do not even inquire if their applicants are doing well in their new organizations, and even when they know, they will not show any emotional attachment to it.

Most recruitment firms, thus, would not allow their applicants to change careers, no matter the challenges the applicants face. All recruitment firms want is their money. So far as they get commissions from the salaries of applicants that were employed through them, they will insist an applicant stay in their current place.

Using recruitment agencies to recruit employees into an organization limits the applicant's knowledge of the prospective employer. Ideally, applicants should learn as much as possible about the organization they wish to work for. The information they receive helps them decide whether to apply for the job or not. However, in some cases, applicants may not know the organization they will be working with until they are officially hired.

Conclusion

The chapter introduced the reader to agencies that have taken the responsibility to recruit for organizations. It explains a recruitment agency as an organization that specializes in matching employers to prospective job seekers. The chapter also makes the reader understand that outsourcing recruitment has been with us for some time and is getting bigger. The challenges that recruitment agencies face in their line of work and how those challenges can be resolved are found in the chapter. The advantages and disadvantages of dealing with recruitment agencies are also explained in the chapter. The next chapter takes the reader on a tour to the top recruitment agencies around the world.

Chapter 4:
Top Recruitment Agencies in the World

Recruitment firms are scattered all over the world. It can be global, continental, or local in nature, depending on where and how they operate. The following is a list of some top recruitment agencies around the world.

	Agency	Specialty	Regions of Operation	Number of Years in Business	Interest
1	DHR Global	1. Consultancy 2. Recruitment	Worldwide	24	1. Nonprofits 2. Healthcare 3.Technology 4. General
2	Approach People Recruitment	1. Consultancy 2. Recruitment	Europe	23	1. IT 2. Life sciences 3. Construction 4. Renewable 5. Energies 6. Marketing 7. Sales 8. Customer service
3	Total	1. Freelancer recruitment	Worldwide		1. Design 2. Business 3. Technology
4	Hays	1. Consultancy 2. Recruitment	Worldwide	50+	1. Architecture 2. Engineering 3. Life sciences 4. Finance 5. IT

5	Manpower	1. Consultancy 2. Recruitment 3. Upskilling	Worldwide	70+	General
6	Artisan Talent	1. Consultancy 2. Recruitment			1. Digital 2. Creatives 3. Marketing
7	Atrium	1. Consultancy 2. Recruitment	Worldwide		1. Creatives 2. Marketing 3. Administrative 4. Customer service 5. Finance and accounting 6. Internship program design 7. Payrolling and IC compliance.
8	Cornerstone Staffing Solutions	1. Consultancy 2. Recruitment	United States of America		1. Accounting and finance 2. Customer service 3. Healthcare 4. IT 5. Engineering fields
9	Creative Circle	1. Consultancy 2. Recruitment 3. Executive recruitment	Worldwide		1. Advertising 3. Marketing 3. Digital 4. Creatives
10	Spherion Staffing Services	1. Consultancy 2. Recruitment 3.Management	United States of America	75+	1. Administrative 2. Clerical 3. Education 4. Customer service

		solutions			5. Accounting and finance 6. Hospitality 7. Engineering 8. Manufacturing.
11	Insight Global	1. Recruitment	USA Canada	20+	1. IT 2. Accounting and finance 3. Engineering 4. Government services.
12	HH Staffing	1. Recruitment 2. Workforce strategies	USA		Drug testing to payroll.
13	Integrity Staffing Solutions	1. Recruitment	USA		1. Technology 2. Industry
14	Roth Staffing	1. Recruitment	USA		1. Industry
15	Robert Half	1. Recruitment	Worldwide	75+	1. Accounting 2. Finance 3. Tech 4. Creative 5. Marketing 6. Legal 7. Administrative
16	Aerotek	1. Recruitment 2. Staffing 3. Strategic outsourcing	Worldwide	40	1. Engineering 2. Scientific 3. Industrial
17	Adecco	1. Recruitment 2. Consultation 3. Staff	Worldwide	25+	1. IT 2. Engineering 3. Finance 4. Legal 5. Science

		training 4. Interview coaching for employers 5. Salary surveys 6. Benchmarking				
18	Randstad	1. Recruitment 2. HR solutions	Worldwide	60+	1. Technology
19	KNF&T Staffing Resources	1. Recruitment	USA		1. General
20	Kelly Services	1. Recruitment	Worldwide	70+	1. Accounting 2. Education 3. Law 4. Science 5. Healthcare 6. IT 7. Engineering 8. Finance
21	MAS Recruiting	1. Recruitment	Worldwide		1. Information Technology 2. Software 3. Robotics 4. Human Resources 5. Operations 6. Marketing 7. Communications 8. RF 9. Wireless 10. Energy 11. Engineering

22	Hasselhoff Recruiter	1. Recruitment	Europe	35+	1. IT
23	Huxley Associates	1. Recruitment	Europe	25+	1. General
24	Chronos Consulting	1. Recruitment 2. Consultancy 3. Structural adjustment programmes	Europe	20+	1. Business 2. Digital industrial solutions
25	Purcon Recruiting	1. Recruitment 2. Client profiling	Worldwide		1. Purchasing 2. Logistics 3. Supply chain 4. Management 5. Quality assurance 6. Manufacturing
26	Experteer Recruiter	1. Recruitment 2. Consultancy	Worldwide		1. Senior level in various industries
27	Artemis Solutions— Talent Search	1. Recruitment 2. Headhunting 3. Talent sourcing strategies	Worldwide	15+	1. Various industries
28	Ajilon Recruiting	1. Recruitment 2. Consultancy	Worldwide		1. Information Technology 2. Engineering 3. Finance and accounting 4. Legal 5. Office support 6. Sales

					7. Marketing, etc.
29	Alderwick Consulting Limited	1. Recruitment 2. Consultancy	Worldwide	25+	1. Commercial 2. Industrial 3. Financial services
30	Lordstone Corporation	1. Recruitment 2. Consultancy 3. Applicant development 4. Successful integration of newly appointed executives	Europe		1. Various industries
31	Expertise Recruitment	1. Recruitment	Europe	14	1. Various Industries
32	Agelix Consulting LLC	1. Recruitment	Worldwide		1. Information Technology 2. Telecom 3. Wireless energy 4. Legal surveillance 5. Manufacturing 6. Educational markets, etc.
33	Hoffman and Associates	1. Executive Search 2. Interim management 3. Board services 4. Management	America and Europe	35+	1. Various industries

		assessment 5. Leadership consulting			
34	Korn Ferry	1. Recruitment 2. Consultancy 3. Executive search	USA	50+	1. Various industries
35	Lucas Group	1. Recruitment 2. Consultancy	USA	50+	1. Various industries
36	Specialized Recruiting Group	1. Recruitment 2. Consultancy	USA	35+	1. Various industries
37	H.I.M. Recruiters	1. Recruitment 2. Consultancy	USA	30+	
38	Kforce Tampa	1. Recruitment 2. Consultancy	USA	60+	
39	TEKsystems		USA	40	
40	AppleOne		USA	59	
41	Rigsby Search Group		USA	21	
42	G-TECH		USA	37	
43	F&C Executive		USA	36	

	Search and Recruiting			
44	FPC National		USA	64	
45	LHH Recruitment Solutions		USA	56	
46	Staff America		USA	24	
47	Crawford Thomas Recruiting		USA	16	
48	Factor Ten Executive Search		USA	27	
49	Inceed Tulsa		USA	22	
50	Gables Search Group		USA	21	
51	Labor Finders		USA	48	
52	LINK		USA	43	
53	Recruiting Connection		USA	20	
54	Vaco		USA	21	
55	A-1 Careers		USA	23	
56	Stout Executive Search		USA	17	

57	HireBetter		USA	17	
58	C. Winchell Agency		USA	31	
59	Michael Page			47	
60	Beacon Hill			22	
61	Ideal Search Group			06	
62	The QualiFind Group			24	
63	Snelling			72	
64	KAS Placement			18	
65	B$Recruiters			30	
66	PACE Bellevue			45	
67	A 1 Personnel			31	

Chapter 5:
Employee Performance Through Effective Recruitment Processes

6.0. Introduction

It is impossible to overestimate the role that recruitment plays in influencing employee performance because it is the cornerstone around which organizations build their workforce. Recruitment serves as a point of entry for organizations to identify, evaluate, and select employees with the competencies, qualifications, and character traits needed to succeed in their positions (Mahapatro 2021). Effective recruitment strategies are important for influencing employee performance and achieving organizational goals in a fast-paced, highly competitive corporate environment where quality talent is a critical factor. The alignment of skills and competencies with job requirements is a key factor in how recruitment impacts employee performance. Recruitment agencies play a vital role by ensuring employees are equipped with the necessary resources and tools to excel in their roles (Mahapatro 2021; Recruitment 101 87 Compton 2009). For instance, hiring a software developer who is proficient in a particular programming language guarantees that he or she can contribute to software development initiatives, increasing output quality and productivity. Additionally, recruitment practices influence employee performance by promoting a culture of engagement and commitment within the organization. Employees are more likely to experience a sense of connection to the organization when they are chosen not only on the basis of their technical talents but also on their alignment with the organization's values and culture (Morgan 2017). Higher levels of job satisfaction, dedication, and discretionary effort are the outcomes of employees' feelings of alignment with the organization's goals and values, which inspires them to perform to the best of their abilities (Morgan 2017). Recruitment plays a crucial role in promoting organizational innovation and adaptability. By expanding the talent pool and attracting individuals with diverse perspectives, experiences, and backgrounds, it fosters creativity and drives innovation within the workplace (Ardi et al., 2024). For instance, hiring employees with a history of creativity and problem-solving abilities may result in the creation of new goods, services, or procedures that boost an organization's ability to compete and expand (Carey et al., 2019). Furthermore, recruitment practices influence employee performance by fostering organizational adaptability and durability. Organizations need to be able to react swiftly to new possibilities and problems in the ever-evolving business environment of today (Breaugh and Starke 2000). Effective recruitment practices help organizations develop employees who are adaptive and flexible enough to deal with change and unpredictability. Hiring employees with a growth mentality and high adaptability abilities, for example, guarantees that organizations may 88 Dr. Arthur Johnson (PsyD) change course and advance in response to technological advancements or market disruptions. Recruitment also impacts employee performance by enhancing the overall quality and capabilities of the workforce. By selecting individuals with the necessary technical skills as well as essential soft skills and attributes for success, recruitment helps build a well-rounded and highly productive team (Tuka 2022). For instance, hiring people with excellent collaboration and communication skills promotes teamwork and cooperation, which improves performance and results for the entire organization. This chapter offers a thorough analysis of the interactions that exist between recruitment practices, employee performance, and ethical considerations in organizations. The chapter covers three primary sections. The chapter examines the conceptual and theoretical frameworks that support the effectiveness of recruitment. It also explores the ways recruitment practices impact employees' output and tackles the obstacles and ethical considerations that are intrinsic to the hiring process.

6.1. Theoretical Framework Supporting Recruitment Effectiveness

The theoretical framework encompasses three theories: person-organization fit (P-O fit), person-job fit, and socialization theory. 1. Person-Organization Fit (P-O Fit) Person-organization fit (P-O Fit) is a theoretical paradigm that places emphasis on how well employees align with the larger organizational culture, values, goals, and conventions (Kaur and Kang 2021). The P-O Fit perspective asserts that the intertwining of employee traits Recruitment 101 89 and organizational context leads to improved employee outcomes (Kaur and Kang 2021). Studies (Herkes et al. 2019; Kooij and Boon 2018) have consistently demonstrated how important P-O fit is for forecasting different organizational outcomes. For example, employees who feel more at home with their organization report higher levels of job satisfaction and organizational commitment. In another study, Naz et al. (2019) mentioned that there is a positive correlation between P-O Fit and employee retention as well as performance.

P-O Fit impacts employee outcomes by reinforcing company identity and values, among other mechanisms. When employees believe that an organization's values and theirs are in alignment, they are more likely to identify with it and absorb its objectives (Kooij and Boon 2018), which boosts their motivation and commitment. In addition, P-O Fit promotes social integration and cohesiveness inside the organization. This is so because employees who are properly intertwined with the culture and values of the organization are more than 90. Dr. Arthur Johnson (PsyD) is likely to form enduring bonds with management and other employees (Kooij and Boon 2018). Furthermore, assessing P-O fit throughout the selection process is an important component of effective recruitment practices that maximize organizational effectiveness and employee well-being. By hiring employees who align with their values, culture, and goals, organizations can enhance job satisfaction, commitment, and performance, while also reducing turnover and absenteeism. Consequently, in today's competitive labor market, incorporating P-O fit considerations into recruitment practices can support an organization's long-term sustainability and success. 2. Person-Job Fit (P-J Fit) Person-Job Fit (P-J Fit) is a model that focuses on how well employees fit into certain job positions. In other words, P-J Fit emphasizes how well an employee's preferences, talents, and competencies match the demands and responsibilities of the job (Ben-Gal 2020). The P-J Fit perspective suggests that better performance, job satisfaction, and retention stem from the alignment between an employee's attributes and the requirements of the role (Chhabra 2015). Studies (Mensah and Bawole 2020; Ben-Gal 2015) indicate that P-J fit is important for predicting employee outcomes in different industries and job functions. For instance, Fisher (2003) discovered that employees report increased satisfaction and performance when they feel more suitable for their tasks. In another study by Hamid and Yahya (2016), the findings indicate that there is a positive correlation between P-J Fit and corporate commitment as well as employee engagement.

P-J Fit impacts employee outcomes by improving task performance and motivation, among other mechanisms. People who have jobs that match their interests, talents, and skills are more likely to feel competent and autonomous, which increases their intrinsic motivation and effort (Edwards 1991). c (Kristof-Brown et al. 2005). Effective recruitment practices that prioritize evaluating P-J fit during the hiring process are important to optimizing employee output and job satisfaction. Organizations can improve employee engagement, commitment, and retention while lowering turnover and associated costs by matching candidates with work responsibilities that correspond with their talents, abilities, and preferences (Edwards 1991). As a result, adding P-J Fit factors to recruitment strategies can improve an organization's performance and overall efficiency. 92 Dr. Arthur Johnson (PsyD) 3. Socialization Theory Socialization theory posits that employees go through a period of adaptation and adjustments when they join a new workplace. During this time, employees learn and internalize the roles, norms, values, and behaviors that are required of them (Bauer and Erdogan 2019). This perspective holds that successful socialization practices help new employees fit in with the organization's culture, which exemplifies commitment, performance, and job satisfaction. Bauer and Erdogan (2019) emphasize the importance of socialization in comprehending the processes of new employee adjustment and organizational socialization. For example, Bauer and Erdogan (2021) mention that employees who go through a more supportive socialization process report higher levels of job satisfaction and organizational commitment. Cable and Vermeulen's (2023) findings show that there is a positive correlation between socialization practices and employee engagement and retention. Socialization influences employee outcomes by fostering the development of social identity and a sense of belonging. As noted by Ashforth and Saks (1996), providing new employees with opportunities to engage with colleagues, receive feedback, obtain support from supervisors, and participate in organizational activities can enhance loyalty, attachment, and other positive outcomes. It can, in turn, improve job satisfaction and commitment. Additionally, socialization improves role clarity and effectiveness by helping new employees grasp their work tasks, responsibilities, and performance standards. This leads to increased productivity and higher performance levels.

Furthermore, optimizing new employees' adjustment and organizational integration requires effective recruitment strategies that place a high priority on socialization and onboarding. Organizations can accelerate the socialization process and foster the development of positive attitudes and behaviors in employees by offering resources, support, and clear information during the transition phase (Bauer and Erdogan 2019). In order to successfully assimilate and retain new employees, recruitment practices should use socialization theory, which will ultimately improve the effectiveness and performance of organizations. In summary, theoretical frameworks such as P-O Fit, P-J Fit, and socialization theory offer important insights into the dynamics of recruitment success and employee performance. Organizations may create more efficient recruitment practices that optimize employee satisfaction, engagement, and productivity. These recruitment practices will help employees align with the organizational and employment context, as well as socialize new employees during their adjustment. Consequently, in order to accomplish organizational objectives and 94 Dr. Arthur Johnson (PsyD) preserve a competitive edge in the labor market, recruitment strategies must incorporate these theoretical perspectives.

6.2. Linking Recruitment Practices to Employee Performance

In this session, three recruitment performance indicators are examined: productivity metrics, quality of work, and job satisfaction and engagement. 1. Productivity Metrics Productivity metrics are important performance indicators for evaluating the effectiveness of hiring practices on employee performance. Brynjolfsson and McAfee (2014) refer to productivity as the ratio of output to input. Put simply, productivity gauges the efficient use of resources to achieve desired results. However, productivity metrics in the context of recruitment refer to a range of quantitative measurements that evaluate how well employee's complete activities, generate outputs, and meet organizational goals (Zairi 2012). One of the main productivity indicators frequently used in recruitment evaluations is output volume. It measures the amount of work employees complete within a given timeframe (Sundstrup et al. 2020; Poister 2008). For instance, high output volume indicates that employees are utilizing their skills and competencies to produce desired outcomes. This reflects positively on the recruitment practices that were used to select the employees who are responsible for increased productivity in an organization. Another productivity indicator used in recruitment evaluations is revenue from sales, especially for employees in sales. Bilan et al. (2020) mention that organizations that use successful recruitment strategies and practices experience higher levels of sales income. This Recruitment 101 95 indicates that recruitment practices have a major impact on sales performance. Organizations can increase revenue and improve overall business performance by choosing personnel with good sales skills, industry knowledge, and customer relationship management abilities (Migdadi 2020). Furthermore, units produced per unit of time is another productivity indicator that evaluates the effectiveness and efficiency of employees in completing tasks or manufacturing goods within a period of time (Zairi 2012). Organizations should anticipate increased productivity in terms of output quantity and quality when priority is placed on recruitment strategies that identify employees with the necessary technical skills, expertise, and experience. Moreover, aside from assessing individual performances, productivity indicators can assess teams' or departmental effectiveness in accomplishing set targets, goals, and objectives. For instance, team productivity indicators could evaluate customer satisfaction ratings, project completion rates, or income or revenue generated by cross-functional teams (Turner 2019). According to Chowdhury et al. (2022), implementing effective recruitment practices that emphasize teamwork, collaboration, and interpersonal skills can enhance team productivity and overall performance. In conclusion, productivity metrics serve as key performance indicators for evaluating the impact of recruitment practices on employee performance. Organizations can evaluate how well recruitment practices select qualified employees who contribute to their productivity by evaluating output volumes, sales revenue generated, units produced per unit time, and team productivity. Therefore, it is necessary to incorporate productivity metrics into recruitment evaluation processes in order to maximize employee performance and meet strategic corporate goals. 96 Dr. Arthur Johnson (PsyD) 2. Quality of Work Quality of work is an important performance metric that shows the caliber and standard of work that employees in an organization accomplish. Quality of work can be quantified in several areas, such as accuracy, thoroughness, innovation, creativity, and adherence to standard practices and guidelines (Sovacool et al. 2018). Evaluating the caliber of work provides information on the effectiveness of recruitment practices in the selection of employees who are consistently delivering high-quality outputs that meet or surpass organizational expectations (Compton 2009). An aspect of quality of work is accuracy, which is the precision and correctness of completed tasks or activities (Ployhart and Moliterno 2011). Employees who demonstrate high levels of accuracy tend to minimize errors, reduce rework, and guarantee the reliability and dependability of delivered goods and services (Ployhart and Moliterno 2011). Higher levels of correctness in job outputs are probably the outcome of effective recruitment practices. These recruitment practices place a priority on selecting top talents with analytical prowess, attention to detail, and conscientiousness. Another important aspect of quality work is thoroughness, which is defined as the completion and comprehensiveness of tasks or projects (Schmitt and Chan 1998). Employees who are thorough in their work show perseverance, diligence, and dedication to reaching goals, which improves organizational performance and efficiency (Southwick, Tsay, and Duckworth 2019). Higher degrees of completeness in work outputs are more likely to result from recruitment practices that prioritize selecting employees with excellent work ethics, problem-solving skills, and task-oriented behaviors (Chandan 2009). Creativity and innovation are also integral components of quality of work, especially in job positions that require ideal generation, Recruitment 101 97 problem-solving, and product development (Alt, Kapshuk, and Dekel 2023). Employees who demonstrate creativity and innovation through novel ideas, processes, products, or services contribute to the expansion and competitiveness of their organizations (Nasifoglu et al. 2020). Fostering an innovative and continuous improvement culture inside the organization requires effective recruitment processes. These recruitment processes evaluate employees' capacity for creative thinking, receptivity to new experiences, and readiness to question the status quo. In addition, sustaining consistency, dependability, and compliance in work outputs depends on adherence to standards and regulations. According to Arjoon (2006), employees who follow organizational policies, processes, and industry regulations and standards help reduce risk, comply with the law, and guarantee customer satisfaction. Furthermore, to ensure adherence to standards and guidelines, recruitment practices place a high priority on selecting employees with integrity, ethics, and professionalism (Doxey 2021). In summary, the quality of work is an important performance metric that represents the excellence and standards of tasks carried out by employees in an organization. Organizations can evaluate the effectiveness of their recruitment practices by assessing factors, such as accuracy, thoroughness, creativity, innovation, and adherence to standards and regulations. It is, therefore, important to integrate quality of work assessments into recruitment evaluation processes in order to optimize productivity and accomplish strategic objectives. 3. Job Satisfaction and Engagement Job satisfaction and engagement are also important performance indicators that reflect the fulfillment, motivation, and dedication of employees to their jobs and organizations (Al-Dalahmeh et al., 2018). 98 Dr. Arthur Johnson (PsyD) Evaluating job satisfaction and engagement provides information on how well recruitment processes select employees that fit with the organization's culture, values, and working environment. In other words, the quality of the recruitment process contributes to the positive attitudes and behaviors of employees in the workplace. Locke (1976) describes the term job satisfaction as the happiness and contentment of employees' feelings about their jobs, work environments, and relationships inside the organization. Happy employees are more likely to be motivated, dedicated, and loyal to the organization. Higher levels of job satisfaction among employees are a result of effective recruitment practices that prioritize selecting employees that fit well with the job roles, team dynamics, and organizational culture. Also, job engagement is a measure of the enthusiasm, commitment, and dedication of employees to their professional activities and meeting organizational targets and goals. According to Bakker and Leiter (2010), motivated employees are more likely to go above their job responsibilities, support team projects, pursue excellence, and engage in continuous improvement. Promoting job engagement among employees necessitates recruitment procedures that place a high value on selecting applicants who share an organization's passion, motivation, and values. Studies (Al-Dalahmen et al. 2018; Bakker and Leiter 2010) show that there is a positive correlation between job satisfaction and engagement and different human and organizational outcomes, such as job performance, lower turnover intentions, and increased organizational commitment. Employees who are content and motivated are more likely to demonstrate increased levels of creativity, innovation, and productivity, which leads to improved organizational performance. Furthermore, Bakker and Leiter (2010) mention that job satisfaction and engagement are important factors that influence the culture of Recruitment 101 99, the organization, and the general employee experience. Employees who find their jobs fulfilling, challenging, and meaningful are more likely to engage positively with supervisors, coworkers, and clients. According to Barak (2022), fulfilled employees contribute to a supportive and inclusive workplace. In order to improve job satisfaction and engagement and foster a positive employee experience, recruitment agencies need to prioritize their evaluation of employees' beliefs, motivations, and career goals. To sum up, job satisfaction and engagement are important performance metrics that reveal employees' attitudes, drives, and dedication to the organization and their jobs. Organizations can evaluate how successfully recruitment strategies select employees who fit well with the job role, team dynamics, and corporate culture by measuring work satisfaction and engagement. This helps to foster positive employee attitudes and behaviors. For this reason, it is important to include job satisfaction and engagement assessments in recruiting evaluation processes in order to maximize staff performance and meet strategic business goals.

6.3. Addressing Challenges and Ethical Considerations

6.3.1 The Common Pitfalls in the Recruitment Process

The common pitfalls in the recruitment process have significance for the performance of employees. The pitfalls discussed herewith include unconscious bias and prejudice, a lack of diversity and inclusion, and a misalignment between job requirements and candidate skills. 100 Dr. Arthur Johnson (PsyD) 1. Unconscious Bias and Prejudice The term unconscious bias refers to "unintentional or implicit bias." It describes the unintended and instinctive prejudices, attitudes, and beliefs that affect decision-making in recruitment and selection processes (Agarwal 2022). According to Adamovic (2022), an interviewer or recruiter can unintentionally prejudice a job seeker without their conscious awareness. The socioeconomic background, age, gender, race, and sexual orientation of job seekers have unintentionally led to prejudice. Unconscious bias has led to subtle discrimination meted out to an individual or a racial group. Unconscious bias significantly affects how employees perform on the job. Recruiters may overlook qualified candidates who do not align with the positive stereotypes associated with specific racial groups. Hence, the recruiters unknowingly favor those groups with positive stereotypes. Unconscious bias can lead to less inclusivity in the workplace and impede an organization's capacity for innovation, creativity, and problem-solving (Thomas and Gabarro 1999). Furthermore, studies (Stephens, Rivera, and Townsend 2020; Ely and Thomas 2001) show that employees who perceive unconscious bias and prejudice in the hiring process may be less motivated, have lower levels of job satisfaction, and be less committed to the organization. The alienation of employees can lead to disengagement and extremely low productivity and performance on the job (Ely and Thomas 2001). According to Hunkenschroer and Luetge (2022), promoting justice and enhancing the efficacy of the recruitment process requires tackling unconscious bias through awareness training, an organized interview process, and diverse selection panels. Recruitment 101 101 2. Lack of Diversity and Inclusion Lack of diversity and inclusion is the act of neglecting to take into consideration and make room for job seekers and employees with different experiences, backgrounds, and perspectives during the recruitment and selection process. Despite the empirical evidence portraying the advantages of inclusion and diversity in the workplace, several organizations find it challenging to implement inclusive hiring practices that attract and retain talent from minority demographic groups. There are several ways in which a lack of inclusion and diversity impacts employee performance. For instance, Smith and Lewis (2022) mention that diverse teams perform better as an organization and make better decisions because they are more creative, flexible, and capable of solving problems. On the other hand, homogeneous teams may experience defects in group thinking and a lack of diverse perspectives, which stifles innovation and restricts the expansion of business development. In addition, employees who experience and perceive the lack of diversity and inclusion in their teams may feel alone, disconnected, and disengaged. This negatively affects work productivity and undermines job satisfaction and happiness. Noon and Ogbonna (2021) assert that enhancing employee performance and organizational success requires prioritizing diversity and inclusion in the recruitment process. 3. Misalignment between Job Requirements and Candidate Skills Misalignment between job requirements and candidate skills occurs when there is a discrepancy between the experiences, qualifications, and training that employers are looking for and what those job seekers have to offer. The misalignment or poor job fit may affect employee performance and job satisfaction. The misalignment between the skills 102 Dr. Arthur Johnson (PsyD) of job seekers and the job requirements has a significant impact on employee performance. Employees may find it difficult to fulfill job requirements and meet expectations for job positions if they have not received substantial training. Job misalignment can lead to increased stress, frustration, and conceived intentions to leave the organization, thereby impacting the effectiveness and productivity of the organization (Cascio and Aguinis 2008). According to Chavadi, Sirothiya, and MR (2022), employees who experience a misalignment between their skills and job requirements are less likely to stay committed to the organization. Also, while job satisfaction may be at an all-time low, engagement with organizational values and goals may be nonexistent. In order for there to be alignment, organizations need to carry out proper job analysis, competent-based assessment, and continuous training and development programs. In summary, it is important to address typical recruitment processes and challenging issues such as unconscious bias and prejudice, a lack of diversity and inclusion, and a misalignment between job seekers and employees' skills and job requirements. By addressing these challenging issues, organizations open up rooms to promote fairness, diversity, and performance in the workplace. Organizations can overcome these challenges by implementing evidence-based strategies and work ethics.

6.3.2. Ethical Considerations in Recruitment

Fairness and equity, honesty and transparency, and privacy and data protection are the ethics that should be considered in recruitment and selection processes. Recruitment 101 103 1. Fairness and Equity The concepts of fairness and equity represent treating all employees equally and impartially, irrespective of their background, traits, or personal ties, throughout the recruitment and selection process (StoneRomero and Stone 2007). Studies (Zhang and Yencha 2022; Nikolaou and Georgiou 2018) indicate that employees' perceptions of fairness throughout a recruiting process have a significant impact on their attitudes and actions. Also, employees make decisions on accepting a job, committing to an organization, and enhancing work performance when fairness and equity are perceived. Thus, maintaining trust and credibility with stakeholders while encouraging positive employee outcomes will require the practice of fairness and equity in recruitment practices. Hence, recruitment agencies should incorporate practices such as standardized selection criteria, equal access to job opportunities, and providing timely and constructive feedback to candidates. 2. Transparency and Honesty In the recruitment process, being transparent and honest is an indication that job seekers and employees are provided with accurate and complete information about their job functions and responsibilities, organizational culture and values, and the selection process. According to Fairholm (1994), being open and honest with job seekers and employees is important to gaining their confidence and reducing perceptions of organizational manipulation. Organizations that place value on their transparent and open-door policies during the hiring process are more likely to attract quality job seekers for long-term engagement with them. Therefore, in order to encourage positive experiences and improve employee performance and retention, it is necessary to maintain an honest and transparent recruitment process. Job seekers and employees 104 Dr. Arthur Johnson (PsyD) should receive honest feedback, realistic job previews, and clear job descriptions. 3. Privacy and Data Protection In the recruitment process, privacy and data protection entail preserving the confidentiality of job seekers' personal information and complying with applicable laws and regulations (Solove and Schwartz, 2020). Organizations should prioritize and guarantee the protection of data and information that pertains to all job seekers and employees in light of the growing use of technology and data analytics in the hiring process. Lee et al. (2011) mention that violating the privacy of job seekers could lead to legal liabilities, reputational damage, and a loss of trust and confidence among stakeholders and employees. Violation of employees' privacy and confidentiality can occur when there is unauthorized access to their personal information by the organizations they represent. Therefore, for the safety and protection of all personal data, organizations need to implement protection measures such as encryption, access controls, and data anonymization (Solove and Schwartz 2020). We can also provide clear privacy policies and consent mechanisms to employees. In summary, addressing the common pitfalls and ethical considerations in recruitment is important for the promotion of fairness and equity, transparency and honesty, and data and privacy protection in the workplace. Organizations can reduce potential hazards and develop inclusive, moral hiring procedures that promote good employee outcomes and enhance long-term organizational effectiveness. Recruitment 101 105 6.4. Conclusion In this chapter, the complex relationship existing between recruitment practices, employee performance, and ethical considerations in organizations has been explored. The chapter begins by examining the theoretical frameworks—person-organization fit, person-job fit, and socialization theory—that underpin recruitment efficiency. These frameworks provide a fundamental comprehension of how hiring procedures correspond with the objectives and principles of the organization. Next, the chapter explored the relationship between hiring procedures and worker performance, going over a number of variables, including output standards, work quality, employee engagement, and job satisfaction. In conclusion, the chapter discussed the difficulties and moral issues that arise throughout the hiring process, pointing out typical mistakes and offering suggestions for advancing privacy, openness, and justice in recruitment practices. In order to promote employee performance and propel corporate success, recruitment is important. Recruiting practices help to increase employee work satisfaction, engagement, and productivity by choosing applicants who fit the organization's values, culture, and job requirements. In addition, proficient recruitment strategies facilitate the establishment of a proficient and competent labor force that fosters creativity, flexibility, and overall organizational efficiency. To improve employee performance and achieve their strategic objectives, organizations must prioritize recruitment as a strategic function and implement ethical and efficient recruitment processes. In order to create evidence-based recruitment strategies, future research and practice in performance management and recruitment should concentrate on integrating theoretical frameworks with real-world 106 Dr. Arthur Johnson (PsyD) insights. Scholars may investigate novel methods for evaluating person-organization fit and person-job fit, including the application of predictive modeling and sophisticated analytics. Furthermore, more research is required to determine how hiring procedures affect employee performance in different sectors, positions, and organizational settings. When it comes to ethical issues in recruitment, practitioners can benefit from taking a proactive stance. Some examples of this include putting in place measures to mitigate bias, encouraging diversity and inclusion, and improving accountability and openness in hiring processes. Overall, researchers can help build more moral and ethical recruitment practices that propel organizations forward in the fast-paced, cutthroat business world of today by deepening their understanding of recruitment practices and how they affect employee performance.

Chapter 6:
Requirements and Expectations of Recruitment Agencies from Job Seekers

7.0. Introduction

Recruitment agencies play a major role in connecting job seekers and organizations, helping to pair skilled job seekers with appropriate job openings. These recruitment agencies utilize many strategies, such as sourcing, screening, and presenting prospective talents to organizations. Recruitment agencies employ these strategies to streamline the hiring process for both job seekers and employers. Additionally, they leverage specialized expertise and extensive networks to match skilled candidates with job opportunities, effectively addressing staffing needs across various industries.

Job seekers must have a thorough understanding of the expectations and prerequisites set by recruiting agencies in order to enhance their likelihood of success in the job market. Recruitment agencies frequently establish precise criteria for selecting candidates, which may include qualifications, experience, and alignment with the culture of hiring organizations. Meeting agency expectations can enhance job seekers' competitiveness and boost their chances of securing attractive roles.

The purpose of this chapter is to provide an understanding of the requirements and expectations of recruitment agencies from job seekers. This chapter seeks to provide job seekers with the necessary knowledge and strategies to connect with recruitment agencies and improve their job-searching efforts effectively. It covers three theoretical models: areas of professionalism, qualifications, adaptability, and industry understanding. It provides an extensive examination of sociological perspectives of employment, recruitment, and recruitment agencies, covering various topics, some of which include types of recruitment agencies, the range of services provided, current trends, and innovations in the recruitment industry.

The chapter offers practical insights and actionable advice for job seekers in today's job market, drawing on a synthesis of current literature and academic discussions. In order to increase their chances of getting rewarding work opportunities, job seekers should strive to gain a comprehensive awareness of the specific expectations that recruitment agencies have. By doing so, job seekers may present themselves as highly attractive candidates.

7.1. Theoretical Framework

7.1. Sociological Perspectives on Employment and Recruitment

This section discusses the sociological perspective on employment and recruitment by examining sociological models like structural functionalism, cultural and institutional factors, and social exchange theory (SET).

A. Structural Functionalism

Structural functionalism, or functionalism, is a macro-sociological model that posits society as a complex system made up of interrelated pieces that cooperate to ensure that there is stability and solidarity (Ormerod 2020; Segre 2016). The theoretical perspective posits that society functions as a cohesive organism, where each part fulfills its duties and role, contributing to the system's survival and overall operation. When applied to the employment system, this theory offers valuable insights into the roles and responsibilities of various institutions and stakeholders in ensuring the efficiency of the labor market. (Schmid 2016). The fundamental tenet of structural functionalism is social integration and consensus (Baert and Da Silva 2010), which indicates that institutions and individuals within a society are linked and work together to accomplish necessary societal roles. This perspective emphasizes the role of labor markets, associations, and regulatory agencies in enabling labor allocation, guaranteeing productivity, and fostering social stability within the employment system.

In order to balance the supply and demand for labor, labor markets are needed to facilitate the effective allocation of human capital across different sectors and organizations. Panayotakis (2014) argues that the principles of meritocracy and competition govern labor markets according to structural functionalism. This means that the labor market rewards people based on their qualifications, skills, competencies, and experiences. Parsons (1951), cited in Scott and Marshal (2009), mentions that meritocratic principles endeavor to assign the most competent individuals to roles that optimize their abilities, ultimately leading to increased economic growth and total production. Keep in mind that organizations play a significant role in the manner in which human activities are structured and coordinated because they represent a fundamental aspect of the employment system. Organizations engage in various activities, including the production of goods and services, providing opportunities for gainful employment, and fostering a work environment that promotes integration and socialization. (Hirst et al., 2023). Robert Merton, in his sentinel study on *bureaucratic structure and personality* in 1940, mentions that organizations are able to distribute roles and responsibilities effectively because of the presence of hierarchical structures and division of labor. As a result, employees are allowed to engage in continuous professional development for their specializations. Emile Durkheim mentions that organizations present opportunities for social contact and cohesion, which allows employees to have an identity and a sense of belonging.

Regulatory agencies, such as the government and labor unions, serve to uphold stability and order in the workplace by instituting guidelines that control labor relations and practices. These institutions play an important role in upholding ethical labor standards, which encompass defining employees' rights and resolving disputes between employers and workers. Regulatory agencies ensure the fair and equitable distribution of resources and opportunities in the labor market through legislation, enforcement, and collective bargaining. This, in turn, fosters social cohesiveness and mitigates inequality. There is existing evidence that highlights the interdependence and connectivity of different labor market components, hence supporting the relevance of different labor components, which is an indication that structural functionalism is applied to employment systems. For instance, there are research findings that show how government policies, demographic shifts, and technological improvements impact labor dynamics, such as wage levels, job openings, and unemployment rates (Autor, 2022; Fossen and Sorgner, 2022).

Comparably, studies on organizational behavior have shown how crucial leadership philosophies, organizational cultures, and organizational structures are influencing employee attitudes, behaviors, and performance results (Cherian et al. 2021; Diana et al. 2021; Gregory et al. 2009). Furthermore, there is ample evidence in the literature about regulatory organizations' role in guaranteeing adherence to labor rules and regulations (O'Rourke 2003). For example, research has demonstrated how anti-discrimination laws, workplace safety roles, and minimum wage laws affect employment practice and results (Carlson et al., 2023; Bartlett et al., 2022). According to Hayter (2015) and Johnston and Land-kazlauskas (2018), labor unions have a positive impact on workers' pay, working conditions, and job security through collective bargaining and representation.

Overall, structural functionalism provides a useful framework for understanding the labor market as a complex social structure that is stable, interdependent, and coordinated. The functionalist perspective explains how society manages the efficient distribution of labor, promotes productivity, and maintains social order. It also analyzes the roles and functions of labor markets, organizations, and regulatory bodies within the economy. By highlighting the interdependence and connectivity of various labor market components and the impact of regulatory agencies, it demonstrates the relevance of structural functionalism to the employment system.

B. Cultural and Institutional Factors

Cultural and institutional factors play a pivotal role in shaping the recruitment industry since they have a strong influence on how organizations find, evaluate, and retain the workforce. Cultural and institutional factors include a broad spectrum of social, political, economic, and legal dimensions that occur differently in various geographical settlements, countries, and organizations. Gaining good knowledge and understanding of the cultural and institutional factors influencing recruitment processes is important for organizations to manage the intricacies of a worldwide workforce and ensure efficacious talent procurement strategies.

The Cultural Factors

The following are the cultural factors:

1. Cultural Values and Norms

Cultural values and norms influence people's beliefs, attitudes, behaviors, and actions in their jobs and careers. For instance, individualism-collectivism, power distance, and uncertainty avoidance are some of the dimensions of Hofstede's theory of cultural dimensions that affect how people view authority, collaboration, and risk-taking at work (Polat 2019). Individualistic organizations may place more emphasis on achievement and autonomy in their recruitment process, while collectivist organizations may place more value on fostering harmony within the group and reaching consensus.

2. Diversity and Inclusion

As organizations attempt to create inclusive workplaces that mirror the demographic diversity of their communities, cultural diversity within societies and organizations has an impact on recruitment processes. Studies show that diverse work teams are more creative, innovative, and adaptable (Webster 2021; Boselie 2014), hence leading organizations to prioritize diversity and inclusion activities in their recruitment strategies. Recruitment practices such as targeted outreach, diversity training, and inclusive language in job ads are some of the strategies aimed at attracting a diverse pool of job seekers.

3. Language and Communication

The differences in language may pose a challenge throughout the recruitment process, especially for multinational organizations or multilingual societies. Effective communication is essential for clearly conveying job requirements, building rapport with candidates, and assessing their qualifications. To bridge linguistic differences, organizations may provide language training for recruiters, translate job advertisements, or conduct interviews in multiple languages (Horn, Lecomte, and Tietze 2020). The following is a diagrammatic representation of the cultural factors:

Diagrammatic Representation of Cultural Factors

Institutional Factors

1. Legal and Regulatory Framework

Legal and regulatory frameworks occur differently in various regions and countries in their influence on the processes of recruitment and selection. According to Thompson (2020), laws and regulations pertaining to labor rights, equal opportunities, and antidiscrimination influence how organizations approach recruitment strategies. Adherence to legal requirements is important in order to prevent legal ramifications and reputational harm that may arise from discriminatory acts, breaches, or labor regulations.

2. Education and Training Systems

Education and training systems play a crucial role in shaping individuals' knowledge and skills. The quality and accessibility of education and training systems influence the availability and suitability of talents for organizations. Organizations may have more access to a trained workforce with the necessary skills and competencies in countries with developed educational systems and vocational training programs. On the other hand, organizations may find it difficult to recruit suitable individuals in areas with limited access to education or training possibilities, and they may need to fund training and development activities.

3. Labor Market Institutions

A number of organizations, including employment agencies, unions, and professional associations, have an influence on the dynamics of the labor market and recruitment practices. Labor union-negotiated collective bargaining agreements, industry standards and norms, and employment laws can impact recruitment processes, pay scales, and working conditions (Moore et al., 2019). Similarly, job boards and employment agencies serve as platforms that facilitate communication between organizations and job seekers through their services and offerings, significantly influencing recruitment strategies. Below is a diagram illustrating the key institutional factors

Diagram of Institutional Factors

Empirical studies shed light on how cultural and institutional factors influence recruitment practices across different contexts. For instance, research findings indicate that there is a positive correlation between cultural values, i.e., collectivism, and preferences for group-based recruitment practices such as networking and employee referrals (Rode, Huang, and Schroeder 2022; Aycan et al. 2007). Also, studies on diversity and inclusion initiatives show that organizations with formal diversity programs have a higher probability of implementing inclusive recruitment procedures and drawing in a pool of talent (Lenton, 2021; Woods and Tharakan, 2021). Legal frameworks and labor market institutions are key factors that influence recruitment processes and outcomes. Research shows that organizations in countries with strict anti-discrimination laws are more likely to adopt fair and transparent hiring practices (Kroll et al. 2021; Bunt 2020). According to the World Health Organization (2021), organizations operating in regions with developed educational systems tend to have more access to a qualified and competent workforce.

To sum it up, cultural and institutional factors have a huge influence on the recruitment process, which in turn shapes how organizations identify, evaluate, and retain talent. Organizations may create more successful and culturally sensitive recruitment strategies to attract different talents and adhere to legal requirements. Organizations can achieve this by considering the cultural values, legal frameworks, and labor market institutions that influence the recruitment landscape. Empirical studies shed light on how these factors affect the recruitment process and emphasize how important it is to understand and adjust to the environment in which organizations operate.

C. Social Exchange Theory (SET)

It is a foundational sociological theory that provides the framework for understanding social interactions (Ahmad et al., 2023). An illustration of social interaction includes those that take place in the context of recruitment relationships through the prism of the exchange of resources, benefits, and costs between individuals or groups. According to Gergen (2021), SET allows people to participate in social interactions with the intent of maximizing their results in relational exchanges while avoiding costs and obtaining rewards. The theory provides valuable insights into the dynamics of interactions between job seekers, recruiters, and employers in recruitment and selection relationships. It emphasizes the reciprocal nature of exchanges and the elements that impact their outcomes.

The concept of reciprocity is integral to SET. Reciprocity holds that people should expect favors and resource exchanges in social interactions. In recruitment relationships, job seekers expect job offers, career growth, and other benefits in return for the time, effort, and resources they invest in job searching, preparing applications, and participating in the selection process. On the other hand, organizations and recruiters invest financial resources in sourcing, screening, and selecting applicants in the hope of finding skilled workers who will support the value, goals, and growth of the organization.

Diagram of Social Exchange Theory in Organisation

Source: Beal, Stavros, and Cole (2013) for their study on effect of psychological capital and resistance to change on organisational citizenship behaviour.

Furthermore, SET highlights that perceptions of equity and fairness influence the behavior and perceptions of people in social exchanges. For instance, job seekers tend to examine recruitment relationships based on perceived fairness in terms of procedural justice and distributive justice (Wang et al., 2020). Procedural justice means the impartiality of recruitment processes, while distributive justice means the impartiality of results (Bustaman et al., 2020). Unfair treatment during the recruitment process, such as acts of discriminatory practices, biased selection criteria, or a lack of transparency, can erode the trust and commitment of job seekers to the organization (Wang et al., 2020). Unfair treatment in the recruitment process leads to a negative impact on the organization because the job seeker may withdraw their intentions and spread negativity about the organization through word of mouth or social media platforms (Lee and Suh, 2020).

Moreover, the theory holds that trust and relational norms are important in promoting effective and efficient exchanges and preserving long-term relationships between parties (Gergen 2021). Building trust in recruitment relationships requires courteous treatment, constant and clear communication, and the fulfillment of commitments and promises (Freiha and Sassine, 2023). Recruiters and employers who exhibit honesty, dependability, and concern for the welfare of job seekers have a greater chance of attracting and retaining top talents because job seekers perceive them as dependable and reliable partners (Kedarnath et al. 2020; Paille 2022).

By illustrating the influence of exchange dynamics on a range of outcomes, such as job satisfaction, organizational commitment, and turnover intentions, empirical research demonstrates the applicability of SET to recruitment interactions (Mohammad et al., 2021). For instance, studies (Mohammad et al. 2021; Bashir and Gani 2020) indicate a positive correlation between job seekers' perceptions of fairness in recruitment processes and organizational commitment and job satisfaction. Similarly, studies (Freiha and Sassine, 2023; Kefharnath et al., 2020) demonstrate a positive relationship between job seekers' intentions to accept job offers and their trust in recruiters and employers.

Moreover, the theory highlights how power dynamics and imbalances shape social interactions. In recruitment relationships, recruiters and employers often hold greater power and control over opportunities and resources than job seekers, potentially leading to unfair exchanges and exploitation. Job seekers' perceived vulnerability and dependence on employers may pressure them to accept unfavorable job offers or endure mistreatment during the hiring process. According to De Bie et al. (2023), fostering positive outcomes and upholding trust and satisfaction among all parties requires efforts to balance power differentials and promote fairness and equity in recruitment partnerships.

Overall, the SET is an important theory that provides valuable knowledge about the dynamics of recruitment relationships by highlighting the reciprocal character of exchanges, the significance of justice and trust, and the influence of power dynamics on outcomes. Through the implementation of SET, organizations may optimize their recruitment procedures, cultivate more robust candidate relationships, and increase the levels of engagement and retention by taking into account the perceptions of employers, recruiters, and job seekers. The relevance of SET to recruitment relationships is backed by empirical evidence, with an emphasis on the roles of reciprocity, fairness, and trust. These concepts—reciprocity, fairness, and trust—play a significant role in influencing the behaviors, attitudes, and actions of job seekers throughout the recruitment process.

7.2. Understanding Recruitment Agencies

It is important for job seekers to understand the different types of recruitment agencies, the services offered, and the trends and innovations that recruitment agencies are adopting.

A. The Different Types and Functions of Recruitment Agencies

Recruitment agencies are important for connecting job seekers with organizations and employers looking to fill vacant positions and individuals looking for work. Employers and job seekers need to understand the different types of recruitment agencies and their functions in order to properly traverse the recruitment industry. This section looks at the two main categories of recruitment agencies:

generalist versus specialist agencies and executive search firms versus temporary staffing agencies.

Generalist versus Specialist Agencies

a. Generalist Agencies

These are recruitment agencies that provide a broad spectrum of activities and services across different industrial sectors, occupations, and employment levels. The client base of these agencies is diverse, from start-ups and small businesses to multinational corporations operating in different industries. Generalist recruitment agencies primarily focus on sourcing job seekers and matching them with open positions across various roles and industries. For example, Randstad offers staffing solutions for a wide range of industries, catering to both entry-level and specialized positions.

Examining generalist agencies involves assessing their reach, versatility, and expertise. Generalist agencies have a wide reach and coverage. Firstly, generalist agencies meet all kinds of staffing demands because they have access to a large pool of job seekers. They also have relationships with a wide variety of organizations operating across different sectors and industries. Secondly, these agencies provide flexibility in meeting the different requirements and demands of the workforce in every organizational context and geographical location. Their staffing supplies range from entry-level jobs to management positions. They also provide skilled and unskilled labor for organizations. Generalist agencies are able to be effective and efficient because they are well-versed in recruitment techniques and methodologies. They have the competence and manpower to provide broad services for both job seekers and organizations.

b. Specialist Agencies

Specialist recruitment agencies focus on niche markets, providing staffing solutions tailored to specific industries, markets, and skill sets. With deep industry expertise and extensive networks, these agencies develop specialized knowledge and proficiency in their chosen fields. Specialist agencies pay particular attention to the specific employment requirements, and as such, they are able to pair job seekers with the specific job function and industry. An example of a specialist agency is Harnham, which is a specialist data and AI recruitment agency that is niche-specific. It provides staffing solutions in the finance, technology, and banking sectors.

The functions of specialist agencies are one: they have a deep knowledge of specific industries; hence, they are able to attract potential job seekers with specialized skills and domain expertise. Two, these agencies use a tailor-based approach to source specific talents and match them with specialized job positions in the specific organization or industry. Thirdly, these agencies provide customized recruitment solutions and advisory services that are exclusive to the requirements of job seekers and organizations.

Tabular Presentation of the Types of Recruitment Agencies

Types of Recruitment Agencies	Generalist	Specialist	Executive Search Firms	Temporary Staffing Agencies
Definition	Offers a broad range of job services for all job seekers irrespective of qualification and skills across all industries	Seek job seekers for specific niches and with specific skills	Seek for job seekers for only senior-level executive positions for organisations	Specialise in providing temporary staffing positions to organisations
Pros	Suitable for all job seekers Services are extensive and accommodating	Access to an extensive network of professionals Excellent	Highly private and confidential Highly skilled	Flexible work Experience across all industries Cost-

	Offers organisation the ability to fill multiple diverse positions at once	sourcing potentials Access to job seekers with specialised skills	agency Access to an extensive network of professionals	effective for agencies
Cons	Lack of access to specialised job seekers Does not offer tailor-made solutions	Fewer job openings Limited in the scope of operations to a specific niche	Expensive to run Limited in operations	Limited career growth Short-term services
Example	Randstad	Harnham	Spencer Stuart	Adecco Group

Executive Search Firms versus Temporary Staffing Agencies

a. Executive Search Firms

Executive search firms specialize in recruiting high-level executives for companies and are also called headhunters or retained search firms. Executive search firms specialize in recruiting senior executives, C-suite professionals, and top management talent for leadership roles. They employ advanced search techniques such as market mapping, headhunting, and confidential searches to identify and attract exceptional candidates who meet an organization's specific leadership needs An example of an executive search firm is Spencer Stuart, which is well-known globally for its services across different industries.

The functions of executive search firms are one: they are focused on recruiting and attracting only top-tier talents for executive and leadership roles within organizations. Executive search firms make use of their broad networks and industry connections to attract and approach potential talents for high-level positions. Secondly, their recruitment and selection processes are discrete and confidential to safeguard the interests of the hiring organization and potential candidates. Thirdly, these firms believe in establishing and maintaining long-term relationships with both job seekers and organizations. They provide individualized services, strategic advisory support, and executive coaching to enable successful placements and leadership transitions.

b. Temporary Staffing Agencies

Temporary staffing agencies play a crucial role in providing companies with flexible workforce solutions. These agencies are also known as temp agencies or staffing firms. These agencies provide organizations with short-term labor needs for seasonal demands, project-based jobs, and contingent and contract-based workforces. Temporary staffing agencies provide organizations with flexible staffing agreements that free them from the long-term commitment that comes with hiring permanent employees, enabling them to quickly scale their workforce up or down in response to shifting business demands. An example of these kinds of agencies is Adecco Group, which is popular for providing talent development, permanent placement, and temporary staffing services to organizations across different industries globally.

Temporary staffing agencies' functions include providing flexible staffing arrangements. Organizations that patronize temporary staffing agencies can modify staffing levels in response to changing business requirements. These agencies also provide on-demand contingent workforce resources through flexible staffing solutions. By handling payroll, labor law compliance, and employee management responsibilities, they act as the employer of record for temporary workers, relieving organizations of the administrative burdens associated with managing a contingent workforce.

Temporary staffing agencies support organizations with project-based, seasonal, or specialized staffing needs. Their project support is for a period of time, and it requires candidates with specialized knowledge.

B. Services Offered by Recruitment Agencies

Recruitment agencies provide a different range of services to improve job seekers' experiences, streamline hiring, and help organizations fill staffing gaps. The importance of recruitment agencies in the acquisition process cannot be overemphasized. Therefore, this section examines the three major services that recruitment agencies offer: candidate sourcing and screening, interview preparation and coaching, and negotiation support and contract management. Each of these services has a vital role in ensuring that the recruitment outcomes are positive, as well as building healthy and long-lasting partnerships between employers and job seekers.

Candidate Sourcing and Screening

a. Candidate Sourcing

Recruitment agencies use different strategies to source job seekers for vacant job positions. These agencies utilize their databases, networks, and web resources to locate qualified job seekers.

Recruitment agencies leverage social media, job boards, professional networks, and industry-specific forums to access a diverse pool of potential job seekers These agencies are actively searching for passive applicants, those who may not be actively looking for work but who have the necessary qualifications, competencies, and skills.

A 2021 study by LinkedIn found that 87 percent of recruiters use the platform to find and screen prospects, demonstrating the usefulness of social media platforms for candidate sourcing. Also, in a study by Indeed in 2020, the findings showed that 64 percent of job seekers use online job boards as their main resource. This also highlights the importance of online platforms in the recruitment efforts of agencies.

b. Candidate Screening

Candidate screening occurs after the candidate sourcing process is completed. Candidate screening involves a rigorous process of screening prospective candidates to assess whether each one is suitable for the position. This process also involves assessing the qualifications, experience, and skills presented by candidates. Other examples of screening include reviewing curricula vitae, conducting initial interviews, performing skills assessments or psychometric tests, and verifying references.

The goal of candidate screening entails making a short list of the best and most qualified candidates for the organization to evaluate for consideration. In a 2021 Glassdoor survey, it was found that 76 percent of recruitment managers believed that the hardest part of the hiring process was vetting applicants for skills relevant to the position. Also, a 2020 Society for Human Resource Management (SHRM) report indicated that 84 percent of businesses perform pre-employment background checks as part of their hiring process to determine a candidate's suitability and reliability.

Prepare for Your Interview with Expert Coaching

a. Interview Preparation

Recruitment agencies help job seekers improve their interview skills and confidence. Recruitment companies offer coaching, tools, and guidance prior to job interviews. This may entail holding practice interviews, advising on how to respond to frequently asked interview questions, sharing details about the organization's culture and values, and providing suggestions for suitable dress and manner. In 2021, CareerBuilder conducted research that showed that 72 percent of employers anticipate that candidates will be able to explain their experiences and talents in an interview effectively. Furthermore, a

TopInterview study in 2020 showed that 58 percent of job seekers experience anxiety or lack of preparation during interviews, underscoring the significance of the interview preparation services offered by recruitment agencies.

b. Interview Coaching

Recruitment agencies may provide job seekers with individualized interview coaching sessions to help them strengthen their communication abilities, clearly state their accomplishments, and highlight any areas of weakness or performance gaps. To help job seekers look more confident and make an impression during interviews, this may entail giving criticism on their general presentation, tone of voice, and body language. Bernhardt (2022) indicates that hiring managers consider nonverbal communication, such as body language and eye contact when evaluating candidates during interviews. In addition, Okolie et al. (2020) showed that candidates who receive coaching during an interview are more likely than those who do not do well and earn job offers.

C. Trends and Innovation in the Recruitment Industry

The recruitment industry is undergoing significant changes driven by technological advancements, shifting workforce demographics, and evolving preferences of both employers and candidates. This section explores three key trends shaping the recruitment landscape: the adoption of technology and automation, efforts to promote diversity and inclusion, and the rise of remote work and virtual recruitment processes. Every trend signifies a fundamental change in recruitment methods, presenting fresh prospects and difficulties for both organizations and recruitment experts.

Adopting and Integrating Technology

The recruiting sector has adopted technological advancements to optimize procedures, increase productivity, and improve the overall experience for job applicants. Recruitment agencies and employers utilize various technologies, such as applicant tracking systems (ATS), artificial intelligence (AI), machine learning, and data analytics, to automate repetitive tasks, identify highly skilled individuals, and make informed decisions based on data throughout the recruitment process. The study conducted by HR Technologist (2021) revealed that 86 percent of HR professionals believe that AI and automation will have a substantial impact on the future of recruitment. In addition, a LinkedIn (2020) study found that 76 percent of talent professionals anticipate a substantial influence of AI on the recruitment process in the next few years. AI-driven solutions are progressively being employed for tasks such as candidate sourcing, screening, and job matching.

Benefits of Technological Adoption and Integration

The benefits include the following:

Efficiency: Technology optimizes recruitment processes, minimizes manual chores, and expedites time to hire, empowering organizations to promptly and economically fill vacant positions.

Precision: AI and data analytics enhance the precision of applicant evaluations by effectively evaluating candidates' talents, experiences, and cultural fit requirements. This results in improved recruiting decisions and decreased turnover rates.

Candidate Experience: The use of technology improves the candidate experience by facilitating customized interactions, clear communication, and effortless application procedures, hence promoting engagement and loyalty among applicants.

Diversity and Inclusion Initiatives

Diversity and inclusion initiatives aim to create a more diverse and welcoming environment for all job seekers and employees. Organizations are becoming increasingly aware of the strategic importance of diversity and inclusion (D&I) efforts in the recruitment and management of talented job seekers. Diverse and inclusive workplaces foster innovation, creativity, and employee engagement, leading to improved corporate performance and a competitive advantage. To attract, retain, and develop diverse talent, recruitment agencies and organizations are increasingly implementing D&I strategies. These strategies aim to mirror the wider variety of society and tackle structural obstacles to equality in the workplace.

McKinsey and Company's (2022) study findings reveal that organizations that embrace diversity and inclusion are more likely to achieve better financial performance compared to organizations that lack diversity. Job seekers seeking employment consider a diverse workforce crucial when assessing job opportunities, as per a 2021 Glassdoor study. This highlights the increasing significance of diversity and inclusion programs in attracting and retaining talented candidates.

Diversity and Inclusion Strategies in Recruitment

Unbiased recruitment practices: Recruitment agencies and organizations utilize impartial recruitment procedures, such as blind résumé screening and structured interviews, to reduce unconscious prejudices and foster just and equitable hiring decisions.

Diverse sourcing channels: Recruitment agencies utilize different sourcing channels, such as job sites that focus on minority candidates, community collaborations, and events specifically aimed at recruiting diverse talent. This approach allows them to reach underrepresented groups and broaden the range of job seekers, thereby enhancing diversity within the applicant pool.

Inclusive employer branding: This refers to the process by which organizations create messaging and initiatives that demonstrate their dedication to diversity, equity, and inclusion. This helps to recruit a wide range of applicants and improve the organization's reputation as an employer.

D. Remote Work and Virtual Recruitment Processes

The COVID-19 pandemic accelerated the adoption of remote work, prompting companies to embrace virtual recruitment methods and remote employment practices. Recruitment agencies and employers now use digital communication tools, video conferencing platforms, and virtual collaboration technologies to conduct interviews, assessments, and onboarding remotely. This enables candidates and hiring teams from different geographical locations to connect and collaborate effectively. Gartner's (2021) recent study revealed that over 80 percent of corporate executives intend to implement remote work policies for their staff even after the epidemic subsides. The finding suggested a notable and enduring trend towards the adoption of remote work arrangements. A study conducted by PwC (2020) revealed that over 50 percent of executives intend to make remote work a permanent option for eligible positions, emphasizing the growing acceptance and normalization of remote work practices.

The Benefits of Remote Recruitment

The benefits of remote recruitment include the ability to access global talents, cost-effectiveness, savings, and flexibility.

Access to global talents: Remote recruitment enables firms to tap into a global talent pool, providing access to top-tier candidates irrespective of their location. This reduces the need to depend solely on local labor markets and enhances workforce diversity.

Cost-effectiveness and savings: Virtual recruitment techniques save on travel, office operations, and logistical arrangements for in-person interviews and evaluations, resulting in financial savings for both organizations and candidates.

Flexibility: Remote recruitment provides a high degree of flexibility for both job seekers and employers, allowing them to adapt to various work preferences, schedules, and lifestyles. It also facilitates smooth communication across different time zones and geographical boundaries.

The recruitment industry is experiencing substantial changes driven by the adoption of technology, efforts to promote diversity and inclusion, and the transition to remote work. These developments offer firms and recruiting experts the chance to improve efficiency, attract a wide pool of talents, and adjust to the changing dynamics of the workforce. To effectively traverse the shifting recruitment market, recruitment agencies, and employers can utilize evidence-based approaches and adopt new solutions. This will help them meet their talent acquisition objectives in a quickly evolving environment.

7.3. Recruitment Agencies' Expectations

The expectations of recruitment agencies from job seekers will be discussed using five fundamental areas: professional and communication skills, relevance of qualifications and experience, adaptability and flexibility, understanding the industries and job market trends, and compliance with agency policies and procedures.

1. Professionalism and Effective Communication Skills

In order to effectively connect job seekers and organizations, recruitment agencies require a high degree of professionalism and effective communication skills. Some of the qualities of a professional candidate are honesty, reliability, and ethical behavior. These qualities are important for establishing credibility and trust with organizations and job seekers alike. Good communication skills are also important for recruitment agencies, which also need to listen intently to prospects' demands, communicate information accurately, and negotiate conditions.

Recruiters demonstrate professionalism in the recruitment process by providing timely answers to questions, respecting confidentiality agreements, and maintaining openness at every stage of the hiring process. According to Breaugh (2024), when recruiters show prospective candidates that they value their time and give candid feedback, even when they are rejected, the professionalism of the recruiter is viewed favorably. Paschina (2023) mentions that there is a positive correlation between professionalism in recruitment and elevated candidate satisfaction and agency trust.

Recruiters who possess effective communication skills may build relationships with prospects, learn about their professional goals, and provide pertinent information about job openings. Studies (Vanamali 2023; Johennesse and Choc 2017; Clampitt 2016; Mutuku and Mathooko 2014) indicate that unambiguous and succinct communication improves candidates' comprehension of job specifications and company culture, resulting in better decision-making and increased work satisfaction. Moreover, recruiters can improve the overall applicant experience and retention rates by addressing candidates' issues and offering customized solutions using active listening skills (Clampitt 2016).

To improve recruiters' professionalism and communication skills, recruitment companies should allocate resources toward ongoing training and development initiatives. Recruiters can negotiate various candidate pools and forge deeper bonds with customers by using training modules that emphasize active listening, conflict resolution, and cultural awareness (Caligiuri 2012). Incorporating technology-enabled communication tools can also improve efficiency and accessibility by enabling smooth connections with candidates across time zones and locales. Examples of these tools include chatbots and video conferencing.

2. The Importance of Qualifications and Experience

Recruitment agencies are responsible for sourcing and selecting candidates with the appropriate training and work experience to meet job specifications and company expectations. Recruiters conduct thorough screenings, interviews, and evaluations to assess the relevance of candidates' experience and skills, ensuring they align with the organization's needs and job requirements. Zhu et al. (2018) mention that to improve job performance and organizational fit, there should be an alignment of job criteria with candidate qualifications and experience. To effectively assess candidates' skills, knowledge, and abilities, recruiters must use competency-based interviewing approaches and standardized assessment tools (Ellis 2014). To reduce the possibility of employing unfit or dishonest applicants, it is also crucial to confirm candidates' qualifications, certifications, and employment history through reference and background checks.

Using technology and data analytics, recruiting agencies can increase the precision and effectiveness of candidate evaluations. According to Zaychenko et al. (2020), applicant tracking systems (ATS) and predictive analytics software can evaluate applications. These software are superior to a candidate's skills to the needs of a position and the use of pre-established standards that pinpoint top talents. Additionally, by adding gamification components to hiring procedures, such as virtual simulations and skills tests, recruiters can analyze candidates' talents impartially while offering candidates interactive and interesting experiences (Buil, Catalan, and Martinez 2020).

Moreover, recruitment agencies must cultivate alliances with academic institutions, professional groups, and business networks in order to remain up-to-date on the latest developments, skill gaps, and industry trends. By collaborating with subject matter experts and industry practitioners, recruiters can better support candidates in career development and upskilling. Working with industry experts allows recruiters to gain valuable insights into evolving job roles, required skills, and available training opportunities. .

3. Adaptability and Flexibility

Adaptability and flexibility are necessary for recruitment agencies to adjust to changing market conditions, client needs, and applicant preferences because they operate in dynamic environments. Flexibility is the capacity to meet a variety of needs and preferences without sacrificing standards or quality, whereas adaptability is the capacity to modify plans and tactics in response to unanticipated obstacles or opportunities.

Adaptability in recruitment means keeping up with changes in the market, technology, and regulations that affect hiring and managing personnel. There have been studies (McDonnell and Wiblen 2020; Cascio 2019; Frank and Taylor 2004) that highlight the importance of ongoing education and training for recruiters to gain new competencies, stay current with industry trends, and adopt creative approaches. Recruitment agencies can increase responsiveness and effectiveness by implementing agile approaches and iterative recruitment techniques like rapid prototyping and experimentation. These techniques allow agencies to test and refine initiatives in real time.

Flexibility in recruiting entails customizing solutions to match the distinct requirements and preferences of organizations and candidates while preserving uniformity and equity in procedures and results. By considering individual preferences and lifestyles, flexible work arrangements—such as remote work options or flexible hours—can attract a broader pool of candidates and enhance retention rates. Additionally, flexibility shows a dedication to developing talent and building long-term relationships with candidates to offer individualized career development plans and support services like coaching.

Using automation and technology, recruiting agencies can improve their operational flexibility and adaptability. Using digital platforms and cloud-based solutions for applicant sourcing, evaluation, and onboarding can simplify procedures, lessen work for administrative staff, and increase scalability (Rudolph et al., 2021). Data-driven insights and predictive analytics can inform proactive recruitment tactics and talent pipelining initiatives to anticipate market changes, labor shortages, and skill gaps (Wang et al., 2018). This increases agility and competitiveness.

4. Understanding Industrial and Job Market Trends

To offer strategic advice and insights to organizations and job seekers, recruitment agencies must be well-versed in market trends, industry dynamics, and emerging technologies. By staying informed about industry-specific information and market intelligence, recruiters can anticipate future skill needs, identify unique talent pools, and advise clients on talent acquisition strategies that align with their business goals. Emphasis has been placed on the value of domain knowledge and industry experience in hiring. Candidates and clients view recruiters who are knowledgeable about industry specific terms, laws, and best practices as more reliable and trustworthy. Furthermore, recruiters can recognize opportunities and problems in talent acquisition and management by having a thorough awareness of market trends, such as demographic shifts, economic indicators, and technological upheavals.

Recruitment agencies can improve their comprehension of industry and job market trends by conducting proactive research, establishing connections, and collaborating with industry groups, thought leaders, and subject matter experts. Recruiters can stay up-to-date on new trends, innovations, and opportunities across a range of industry events, conferences, and webinars (Rankine and Giberti 2020). In addition, recruiters, organizations, and job seekers collaborate easily through social media platforms and online forums for knowledge sharing and community participation (Nayak, Nayak, and Jena 2020).

Investing in training programs and professional development will also help recruiting agencies provide their recruiters with industry-specific information and abilities. Recruiters can improve their knowledge and reputation in specific fields by participating in workshops, seminars, and certificate programs on subjects including talent mapping, market research, and regulatory compliance (Rankine and Giberti 2020). Creating an environment that values ongoing education and information exchange among team members motivates recruiters to remain inquisitive, flexible, and sensitive to changing market and candidate demands.

5. Compliance with Agency Policies and Procedures

Recruitment agencies are required to comply with agency policies, processes, and industry regulations as they are subject to legal and ethical standards that regulate their activities. Adherence to agency regulations guarantees uniformity, lucidity, and equity in hiring procedures, preserving the rights and concerns of customers and applicants while mitigating legal and reputational hazards for the agency.

The rules and procedures of the agency delineate the standards and methods for carrying out recruitment-related tasks, such as locating, screening, evaluating, and assigning candidates. Standardizing hiring procedures is important for maintaining decision-making impartiality, dependability, and validity (Cascio and Aguinis, 2005). Chapman et al. (2018) mention that following defined procedures and quality control standards, such as organized interview guides, evaluation standards, and documentation, improves the legitimacy and dependability of hiring processes.

Furthermore, in order for recruitment agencies to preserve moral principles and safeguard the rights and privacy of both organizations and job seekers, compliance with legal and regulatory regulations is important. Strict adherence to laws and regulations pertaining to anti-discrimination, data security, and equal employment opportunity is necessary to avoid discriminatory practices, privacy violations, and legal ramifications (Dunn and Woodruff 2017). When handling sensitive candidate information, using strong data management and security measures, such as encryption, access limits, and data retention policies (Lengnick-Hall et al. 2019), helps assure confidentiality and integrity.

Recruitment agencies may promote a culture of ethics and compliance by offering thorough instruction and training on company regulations, legal obligations, and professional standards. Recruiters can effectively manage ethical dilemmas, conflicts of interest, and compliance challenges with the use of ethics training programs, case studies, and scenario-based simulations (LeDoux and Ramsay 2016). According to Trevino et al. (2014), creating unique channels for reporting challenges, such as grievance procedures or anonymous hotlines, promotes accountability and openness in maintaining recruitment agencies' principles and values.

In summary, recruitment agencies need to maintain the highest levels of professionalism, ethics, and compliance if they are to satisfy their clients (organizations), job seekers, and regulatory bodies. Recruitment agencies can build credibility and foster long-term relationships with stakeholders by prioritizing professionalism and strong communication skills, ensuring candidates' experience and qualifications are relevant, demonstrating adaptability and flexibility, staying informed about industry and job market trends, and adhering to agency policies and procedures. Recruitment agencies may successfully manage talent acquisition and achieve long-term success in the recruitment market by adopting technology, providing continuous training, and having ethical leadership.

7.4. Application Process and Documentation

In this session, we explore the areas of résumé and CV writing and formatting guidelines, cover letters and personal statements, portfolio development and presentation, and verification of qualifications and references.

A. Résumé or Curriculum Vitae (CV) Writing and Formatting Guidelines

The résumé is the most important document in the job application process because it provides brief but deep details of a job seeker's educational qualifications, work experiences, skills, strengths, achievements, hobbies or interests, and references. To create and write an effective résumé, meticulous attention to content, structure, and presentation must go into writing an effective résumé.

A1. Content

A résumé's contents include the following:

Contact information: This includes the full name of the applicant, home or office contact address, email address, and phone number. It sits at the top of the résumé.

Professional Summary: This section provides a summary of the applicant's strengths. It discloses career goals and salient abilities the applicant has that are pertinent to the job role. It is usually brief—less than one hundred words—but detailed.

Education: Here, the applicant lists the degrees and certifications he or she has received over the years in reverse chronological order. It follows in order the names of the institutions, degrees obtained, and graduation dates.

Work experience: This section utilizes action verbs and quantitative outcomes. The details of the work experience subsection include a description of the relevant work experience in detail. State the organization's name, job title, period of employment (month and year), key responsibilities, and accomplishments.

Skills: Here, applicants' emphasis is on their transferable, soft, and relevant technical skills in relation to the job sought after.

Achievements and awards: Here, applicants mention their accomplishments, publications, certifications, and awards that attest to their authenticity and quality.

Professional development: This includes relevant training, workshops, or conferences attended. The applicant's engagement in ongoing learning and skill enhancement is demonstrated.

A2. Formatting

The résumé's formatting requires:

Consistency: This entails ensuring that the résumé displays consistency in using the same font type, size, and spacing.

Readability: This requires the use of a clear and readable font type. Some of the most used font types are Times New Roman and Arial. There should also be plenty of white space.

Bullet points: To highlight key achievements and responsibilities, the information on the résumé should be presented in concise bullet points.

Reverse chronological order: To highlight the most current and pertinent events, it is important to arrange the sections and entries in reverse chronological order.

Length: The résumé should be focused and concise. The length should be no longer than two pages for entry-level to mid-level career positions.

Customize each résumé to align uniquely with the job opportunity or job interest. This can be done by emphasizing the qualifications, relevant experiences, and skills.

A3. Presentation

Present the CV using the following:

Visual appeal: To develop a visually appealing document, use a consistent formatting style and a clean, professional design.

Keyword optimization: To improve searchability and make the job description more compatible with Applicant Tracking Systems (ATS), include pertinent keywords from the job description.

Proofread the résumé to avoid spelling errors, grammatical mistakes, and punctuation errors.

Customization: Every résumé should be customized to fit the job description. The emphasis should be on the experiences and skills fitting for the job position.

Online presence: To provide transparency and give more information about one's work, there is a need to include links to professional websites, portfolios, or online profiles.

Gilch and Sieweke (2021) mention that customizing a résumé and aligning it with job requirements are more likely to capture the attention of recruiters and gain an interview invite. Furthermore, Keaveney and Woodcock (2017) show that the efficacy of a résumé is enhanced when it has a clear and concise presentation, while a cluttered and confusing layout reduces the efficacy of the résumé.

B. Cover Letters and Personal Statements

Cover letters and personal statements present job seekers with the opportunity to introduce themselves and contend for the job, which means providing good reasons why they are the best candidates for the job. Cover letters and personal statements provide applicants with an opportunity to showcase their qualifications and motivation while explaining their skills and accomplishments. A well-written cover letter requires attention to detail, originality, and an emphasis on how the organization's values and needs align with the applicant's personal goals.

B1. Content

The contents of a cover letter and personal statement should include the following:

Introduction: It is important to begin strong in the opening sentence, as it will capture the attention of the reader. The introduction will state the statement's purpose or intent.

Interest and fit: It is also important for applicants to genuinely express their desire to work with the company by demonstrating knowledge and familiarity with the culture, goals, and core values of the organization.

Relevant experience: Here, applicants should emphasize the most important accomplishments, abilities, and experiences that fit the job description and demonstrate the reason why they should be considered for the job position.

Motivation: Applicants should be clear on the reasons why they are applying for the job. Here, the aims and career goals and how the role fits into long-term goals should be stated.

Value proposition: The applicant should emphasize the distinct contributions and value offered to the organization and support it with relevant examples.

Closing statement: In the closing statement, summarize your interest in the role, express your gratitude for the opportunity, and issue a strong call to action (such as asking for an interview).

B2. Structure

The structure includes the introduction, body paragraphs, and conclusion. The explanation is as follows:

Introduction: In the letter or statement, give a brief but detailed introduction of yourself and the purpose of the letter.

Body paragraphs: Provide thorough illustrations and proof to back up your credentials and objectives. In closing, restate the main ideas, convey your excitement about the chance, and extend an invitation for more correspondence.

Conclusion: In closing, restate the main ideas, convey your excitement about the opportunity, and extend an invitation for more correspondence.

B3. Tone and Style

A cover letter and personal statement should have the following tone and style:

Professional tone: Ensure that the letter has a professional tone by avoiding using slang and jargon in the writing.

Conciseness: The letter should be focused and straight to the point. Include only the most important.

Personalization: Avoid using generic or template-based text. Every job opportunity requires a unique letter. Therefore, for every job interest, a new letter should be written with it.

Authenticity: Be genuine, sincere, and natural in your writing because it endears the reader's interest.

Keaveney and Woodcock (2017) mention that personalized cover letters and well-written ones have a significant impact on recruiters' opinions of job seekers. In another study, DeCenzo and Robbins (2016) found that well-written cover letters show a thorough comprehension of the organization's requirements and clearly state how job seekers' qualifications may meet those demands. Furthermore, Whitmore (2017) mentions the importance of cover letters in communicating job seekers' goals and cultural fit, which are important factors in recruitment and selection decisions.

C. Developing and Presenting Your Portfolio

A professional portfolio is a collection of the actual evidence and examples used to showcase a candidate's experience, competencies, skills, and accomplishments for professional development and employment (Michelson and Mandell, 2023). A professional portfolio can be in hard copy or digital media. It is simply an avenue for candidates to systematically organize and position themselves for employment.

C1. Content

A professional portfolio's contents include the following:

Introduction: It provides a synopsis of the goals, contents, and applicability to the position or sector.

Work samples: This includes the different projections, work samples, or case studies that highlight the candidate's accomplishments, expertise, and relevant skills to the position or sector.

Descriptions and annotations: In order to aid readers in understanding the importance and applicability of the content, there is a need to offer background information, justifications, and thoughts on each work sample.

Achievements and awards: Here, the candidate highlights any notable achievements, prizes, or recognitions that they have won for excellence at work or services.

Testimonials and recommendations: It is necessary for candidates to provide testimonials or endorsements from co-workers, managers, or customers who can vouch for their skills and moral integrity.

Professional development: In order to demonstrate a commitment to continuous progress, candidates must provide evidence of continuing learning and development initiatives using credentials, training courses, and professional memberships.

C2. Format and Presentation

Visual design: Here, candidates use attention to detail, consistent branding and clear organization to create a visually appealing layout.

Digital accessibility: Ensure that digital portfolios have an intuitive interface, are navigable on different platforms and devices, and are easy to use.

Multimedia elements: In order to improve engagement and effectively demonstrate abilities and accomplishments, it is important that multimedia components such as pictures, videos, and interactive information are included.

Professionalism: Keep the portfolio looking polished and professional at all times with well-written content and perfectly formatted pages.

Customization: Adapt the portfolio to the particular position or sector, highlighting accomplishments, experiences, and pertinent abilities that meet the requirements and expectations of the intended audience.

In the creative and technology sectors, professional portfolios are effective in proving concrete evidence of individuals' skills and competencies (Lu 2021). Employers value portfolios as a way of evaluating job seekers' inventiveness, problem-solving skills, and attention to detail (Michelson and Mandell, 2023). This makes portfolios a useful addition to conventional résumés and interviews. In addition, Jones and Shelton (2011) mention that professional portfolios help to differentiate job seekers and showcase their unique value proposition in competitive job markets.

D. Verification of Qualifications and References

Verifying job seekers' qualifications and references during the recruitment process is crucial for determining their suitability for the position and ensuring the accuracy of their credentials. Verification processes help employers avoid hiring unqualified job seekers, assure regulatory compliance, and make well-informed hiring decisions.

D1. Qualification verification

Educational background: Job seekers' academic credentials, degrees, certifications, and diplomas from accredited institutions should be verified using degree verification services or direct communication with educational institutions.

Professional certifications: Use online verification tools, licensing authorities, or appropriate certifying organizations to confirm candidates' professional qualifications, licenses, and credentials.

Employment history: Verify candidates' employment histories, job titles, start and end dates, and important duties by calling past employers directly using employment verification services or running reference checks on them.

Skills and competencies: Evaluate candidates' skills, competencies, and abilities through skills assessments, work samples, or technical reviews to verify the proficiencies and qualifications provided.

D2. Reference Verification

Reference checks: To confirm candidates' work performance, moral character, and appropriateness for the position, get in touch with the references they provided. The references could be coworkers, mentors, or previous supervisors.

Professional recommendations: To confirm a candidate's competence and credibility, get professional recommendations or endorsements from people who are familiar with their work, such as clients, collaborators, or colleagues in the industry.

Character assessment: Examine candidates' references and testimonies to determine whether they are in line with the company's principles and culture of the company by examining their references and testimonies. This will help you determine their honesty, dependability, and character.

Third-party verification: To guarantee due diligence and adherence to legal requirements, perform thorough background checks on candidates' credentials, references, criminal histories, and other pertinent information using third-party verification services or background screening organizations.

According to Fein (2012), rigorous verification processes are necessary to guarantee the veracity and correctness of applicants' qualifications and references. Given its crucial role in risk management and talent assessment, organizations rank the verification of credentials and references as one of their top concerns throughout the recruitment process (Nankervis et al., 2019). Furthermore, Vardarlier (2020) discussed the advantages of utilizing automated verification tools and technologies to increase accuracy and efficiency and streamline the verification process when screening and selecting candidates.

7.5. Interview Preparation and Performance

Interview preparation and performance are important for job seekers as well as recruitment agencies. Hence, job seekers need to understand the types of interviews and assessment methods, research of employers and industries, techniques for answering behavioral and situational questions, professional etiquette and body language, and post-interview follow-up and feedback-seeking.

A. Types of interviews and assessment methods

Interviews are the most important part of the hiring process. It allows employers to assess job seekers' qualifications, skills, and suitability for the position. Assessing the competencies of job seekers and their suitability for the position involves using different types of assessment methods and interviews. The types of interviews include the following:

Structured interviews

Structured interviews consist of a prepared set of questions that are predetermined and centered on specific job-related behaviors or competencies (Leutner, Akhar, and Chamorro-Premuzic, 2022). Interviewers ask all potential job seekers the same questions. The benefits of structured interviews are that they promote impartiality and are a consistent form of evaluation. It lowers bias and allows recruiters to make direct comparisons with potential job seekers. The disadvantage is that it is not flexible, which could make it difficult to establish rapport. It also limits the ability to explore the responses of candidates during the interviews; hence, the evaluation may not be in-depth. Leutner et al. (2022) mention that structured interviews yield more accurate job performance forecasts than unstructured interviews due to their higher validity and reliability.

Unstructured Interviews

Unstructured interviews are characterized by the use of open-ended questions that promote a conversational style of interaction between the interviewer and potential job seeker (Gerson and Damaske, 2020). This approach enables interviewers to explore a wide range of interests and topics. The advantage of this interview style is its flexibility, allowing both the interviewer and the candidate to connect and gain a deeper understanding of the candidate's interest in the position.

It also allows the interviewer to evaluate the interpersonal skills and cultural fit of the job seeker. The drawbacks are that it is subjective; hence, there may be irregularities in the assessment, and it can lead to prejudice and bias. It also has lower dependability, and it lacks the ability to make comparisons among job seekers. Gerson and Damaske (2020) mention that unstructured interviews are more prone to interviewers's biases and idiosyncratic judgments. Unstructured interviews have worse validity and reliability than structured interviews (Chauhan, 2022).

Behavioural Interviews

Behavioral interviews are used to analyze a job seeker's prior experiences and behavior as a means of anticipating their future performance (Gerson and Damaske 2020). These types of interviews incorporate the use of the STAR (Situation, Task, Action, Result) method to extract specific examples of persistent abilities and competencies. The benefit of behavioral interviews is that they improve predictive validity and alignment with job criteria by offering proof of job seekers' aptitudes, accomplishments, and problem-solving skills. This type of interview is a disadvantage for applicants with nontraditional or limited backgrounds because it requires job seekers to have relevant experiences, which it uses in its evaluation process. Studies (Affum-Osei and Chan 2024; Bhargava and Assadi 2023) show that behavioral interviews outperform traditional interviews when it comes to predicting job success, especially for occupations that are difficult and have high risks.

Assessment Centers

Assessment centers consist of a sequence of organized drills, role-plays, and simulations intended to assess job seekers' proficiencies in problem-solving, leadership, and communication in simulated work settings (Pattnail and Padhi 2021). The benefit of assessment centers is that they provide chances for comprehensive evaluation of job seekers' abilities, attitudes, and interactions in realistic situations, improving predictive validity and locating high-potential individuals (Pattnail and Padhi 2021). The disadvantage is that assessment centers require a lot of resources and time. It also requires collaboration and careful planning, as well as adequate knowledge of assessment design and evaluation. According to Thorton and Byham (2013), assessment centers show strong predictive validity for work performance across a variety of job types and organizational levels.

Technical Interviews

Technical interviews are used to evaluate a job seeker's knowledge, talents, and problem-solving skills in specific technical domains or areas of expertise that are pertinent to the position, including coding, engineering, and data analysis (Robinson and Nolis, 2020). The advantage of a technical interview is that it enables interviewers to carry out a thorough assessment of job seekers' technical expertise, inventiveness, and capacity to apply theoretical knowledge to real-world issues. The drawback is that it may create unfair assessment disparities by limiting job seekers who have less access to formal education or technical resources. Robinson and Nolis (2020) suggest that technical interviews are useful for locating job seekers who possess the technical know-how required for specialized positions like data science or software development.

Bear in mind that the different types of interviews and evaluation techniques provide special benefits and factors to take into consideration when assessing job seekers' qualifications, skills, and suitability for a position. Employers can improve the validity, reliability, and fairness of their selection processes by choosing suitable methods based on job requirements, corporate culture, and intended outcomes.

B. Conducting Research on Employers and the Industry

In order to demonstrate expertise, passion, and alignment with corporate aims and values, job seekers should thoroughly investigate potential employers and sectors before their job interview. Therefore, it is important to investigate the organization, industry insights, organizational culture, recent news and development, and networking and information interviews.

Organizational Overview

When exploring an organization, one has to look at its mission and values, products and services, history, and milestones.

Mission and values: To determine whether an organization's mission, vision, and core values correspond with one's personal values, interests, and motivation.

Products and services: To show that you comprehend the organization's business model and competitive environment, familiarize yourself with its products, services, and target markets.

History and milestones: Job seekers need to examine the organization's past, significant events, and accomplishments to put its development and expansion trajectory into perspective.

Industry Insights

The industry insights include market trends, the competitive landscape, and the regulatory environment.

Market trends: Stay up to date with market dynamics, industry trends, and emerging technology to foresee possibilities and obstacles for the company.

Competitive landscape: To identify areas of differentiation and unique selling points and evaluate market positioning, rivals, and strategic efforts.

Regulatory environment: To evaluate risk factors and regulatory ramifications and comprehend industry standards, compliance requirements, and regulatory frameworks that are important to the organization's operations.

Organizational Culture

Employee reviews and feedback: Explore employee reviews, testimonials, and feedback on platforms such as Glassdoor or LinkedIn to gain insights into organizational culture, work environment, and employee satisfaction.

Diversity and inclusion initiatives: To evaluate the company's dedication to promoting an inclusive and equitable workplace, look into employee resource groups, diversity and inclusion initiatives, and corporate social responsibility programs.

Recent News and Developments

This involves examining press releases and media coverage as well as analyzing the financial performance of organizations.

Press releases and media coverage: Read up on company announcements, industry recognition, and strategic alliances by reviewing press releases, news stories, and media coverage.

Financial performance: To assess the company's financial standing, future growth potential, and performance indicators, examine financial reports, earnings calls, and investor presentations.

Networking and Informational Interviews

This involves the following:

Professional network: Job seekers can use alumni connections, industry associations, and professional networks to get tips, recommendations, and insights from current or previous employees.

Informational interviews: Conduct informational interviews with employees or industry professionals to gain insider perspectives, advice, and tips on navigating organizations.

According to Gilch and Sieweke (2021), job seekers who show that they are knowledgeable about an organization's background, products, and market trends are thought to be more engaged, driven, and dedicated to the organization's objectives. Also, Davies et al. (2023) found that candidates are more likely to get favorable interviewer assessments and job offers if they perform in-depth research and ask thoughtful questions during the interview process.

Furthermore, Wanberg, Ali, and Csillag (2020) emphasized the importance of investigating organizational values and culture during the preparation for the interview. This is so because a job seeker's goal, values, and beliefs need to align with an organization's values and culture.

C. Techniques for answering behavioral and situational questions

Interviewers frequently use situational and behavioral questions to assess a job seeker's aptitude for problem-solving and decision-making, as well as their prior experiences. Job seekers can perform better and demonstrate their suitability for the position by practicing effectively and answering the questions strategically using methods such as STAR, PAR, CAR, BARS, and SOAR. Below, we will explain these acronyms:

STAR Method

STAR stands for Situation, Task, Action, and Results. The situation requires describing the situation or context in which the experience occurred. It involves providing background information and establishing the groundwork for the story. The task requires the job seeker to clearly define their role and responsibilities, outlining the specific task or objective they were responsible for in the given scenario. In the action phase, job seekers must describe the steps they took to address an issue or complete an assignment, focusing on their decisions, actions, and methods for resolving conflicts. The result requires job seekers to provide an overview of the consequences or outcomes of their activities, emphasizing personal accomplishments, insights, and organizational contributions.

PAR Method

PAR stands for Problem, Action, and Results. The problem entails providing a description of the difficulties, challenges, or barriers one faced in a particular scenario while emphasizing the importance and context of the problem. The action requires describing the steps followed to solve the issue, together with the methodology for problem-solving and rationale for making decisions. The results require job seekers to talk about the consequences or results of their actions, highlighting how their efforts affected the problem's resolution, the accomplishment of their objectives, or the creation of favorable results.

CAR Method

CAR stands for challenge, action, and result. Job seekers provide an explanation of the opportunities, challenges, and objectives they encounter in a specific circumstance, emphasizing its complexity, urgency, or significance through challenge. The action requires outlining the steps taken to overcome the obstacles or seize the opportunity, while also highlighting the initiatives, inventiveness, and leadership taken. The outcome requires a job seeker to share the results or outcomes, emphasizing quantifiable achievements, enhancements, or contributions to the prosperity of the company.

BARS Method

The acronym BARS stands for Behavioral Anchored Rating Scales. Job seekers are expected to give precise instances or anecdotes from prior encounters of important traits, abilities, or behaviors relevant to the position. Job seekers are also expected to quantify the results or outcomes using metrics, numbers, or percentages to demonstrate their impact and effectiveness. The BAR method encourages candidates to contextualize their actions and decisions by explaining the challenges, limitations, and circumstances they face. .

SOAR Model

The SOAR model is situation-action-outcome-reflection. Job seekers should provide a detailed account of the specific circumstance or setting in which the event took place, including any pertinent background details. Through the action, job seekers are expected to describe the steps they took to deal with the circumstance, issue, or obstacle, along with their reasoning, process, and standards for making decisions. Additionally, the outcomes of their actions should be discussed, emphasizing accomplishments, lessons learned, and how these experiences may influence future behavior or decision-making. In reflecting on these experiences, a summary of key events should be provided, along with a focus on important lessons, surprising discoveries, and potential areas for growth. This will show self-awareness and a growth mindset.

According to Filch and Sieweke (2021), behavioral interviews yield specific instances of prior behaviors and experiences related to the job, making them more predictive of job performance than standard interviews. Gerson and Damaske (2020) found that because structured behavior interviews concentrate on specific skills and behaviors that are essential for success in the workplace, they have higher validity and reliability than unstructured interviews. Bergelson, Tracy, and Takacs (2022) highlight the importance of applying standardized rating scales and evaluation criteria to improve objectivity and consistency when evaluating job seekers' answers to situational and behavioral questions.

D. Professional etiquette and body language

Professional etiquette and body language are important when it comes to influencing the position of the job seeker's impressions, perceptions, and interactions during the interviewing process. Using proper manners and body language to convey confidence, professionalism, and interpersonal skills can have a favorable impact on interview results and perceptions. Job seekers should dress professionally and maintain a well-groomed appearance. Additionally, handshakes and greetings should be polite and firm, while posture and body language should convey confidence. Attentive listening, effective use of nonverbal cues, and a clear, confident tone of voice are also essential in making a positive impression.

Dress and Appearance

Job seekers must dress appropriately for the interview. Pick and wear outfits that are clean, well-fitted, and comply with the organization's dress code and industry standards. Also, the hair should be neat, have clean nails, and use minimal accessories to avoid distraction. In other words, job seekers should practice proper personal hygiene.

Handshakes and Greetings

Handshakes should be confident and firm, not aggressive. Job seekers should have a warm smile that portrays confidence and professionalism. Always make eye contact. Job seekers should be kind enough to extend a warm welcome to interviewers, using their names if known. Express gratitude to the interviewers for selecting you for the interview.

Posture and Body Language

While in the interview, job seekers should sit upright with their shoulders back and feet firmly planted on the floor; this conveys a sense of assurance and focus. Also, job seekers should endeavor to keep their arms and legs straight to prevent giving off the impression that they are uncomfortable or being defensive. To demonstrate demonstrative involvement, sincerity, and attentive listening, job seekers should always maintain eye contact with interviewers.

Active Listening and Nonverbal Cues

Job seekers should use non-verbal cues such as nodding and smiling to establish rapport and connection. Nodding and smiling are effective tools used to convey agreement, understanding, and interest in the topic at hand. Mirroring is another tool that job seekers can use to create a connection and show empathy. Therefore, a job seeker can mimic the interviewer's motions and body language subtly. Examples of nonverbal clues that can be used to reinforce key points and emphasize important information are head nods, facial expressions, and gestures.

The tone of Voice and Speech

Job seekers should speak with clarity and confidence to project professionalism, authority, and credibility, while maintaining an appropriate volume, pace, and tone. Additionally, using upbeat and positive language helps create a strong impression, conveying enthusiasm, motivation, and genuine interest in the job opportunity. Wood (2012) mentions that body language and nonverbal clues shape impressions and interpersonal perceptions during first interactions, affecting assessments of competence, likeability, and trustworthiness. It is important to pay attention to professional etiquette and body language in interview settings. McCarthy and Cheng (2018) found that interviewers' perceptions of job seekers' warmth and competence based on nonverbal clues affect hiring decisions and results. Furthermore, Lacoboni (2009) emphasized the influence of mimicking and mirroring behaviors on rapport-building and social bonding in social encounters. The study findings show that subtle nonverbal clues may improve communication efficacy and interpersonal connection.

E. Post-Interview Follow-Up and Feedback Seeking

In order to show professionalism, gratitude, and ongoing interest in the position, job seekers should actively participate in post-interview follow-up and feedback-seeking activities after the position. Job seekers should also aggressively seek out insightful comments and advice for both professional and personal development.

Thank You Notes

Expressing gratitude through thank-you notes is essential. Thank you notes should be prompt, specific, and show gratitude.

Promptness: Job seekers should send thank-you notes or emails within twenty-four to forty-eight hours following the interview. Job seekers in the note or email should express appreciation for the recruiters' time, insights, and thoughtfulness.

Specificity: Job seekers should make specific references to elements of the interview, such as important conversation points, common interests, or standout moments, to personalize the message and bolster favorable impressions.

Gratitude: This should be shown by expressing a genuine thank you for the interview opportunity. Job seekers should reiterate their excitement and interest in the role and organization.

Professionalism and Etiquette

This can be shown by being polite and respectful, concise, and paying attention to details (proofreading) in the email or other means of communication.

Politeness and respect: In all communications, job seekers should keep their tone civil and courteous. There is no need to be too personal or causal, as these could come across as unprofessional.

Conciseness: Job seekers should respect interviewers' time and attention by keeping follow-up messages succinct and targeted while also successfully communicating important points and attitudes.

Proofreading: To ensure professionalism and attention to detail, carefully review follow-up emails and thank-you letters for spelling, grammatical, and formatting mistakes.

Feedback

In seeking feedback, the notes or email should be constructive, a feedback request, and professional.

Constructive inquiry: Job seekers should express enthusiasm and continuous interest in the opportunity while politely asking about the status of the recruiting process and the decision-making schedule.

Feedback request: Job seekers should show their willingness to learn and grow professionally by asking for comments on interview performance, strengths, opportunities for growth, and general fit for the position.

Professionalism: When asking for feedback, job seekers should present themselves professionally and helpfully, emphasizing possibilities for growth and practical insights above criticism or defensiveness.

Persistence and Patience

Job seekers can display their persistence and patience by engaging in follow-up protocol, respecting boundaries, and having patience.

Follow-up protocol: Job seekers should respect interviewers' schedules and preferences by adhering to the proper follow-up rules and timetables and by practicing perseverance and proactive engagement.

Respect boundaries: Job seekers should be mindful of interviewees' limits and communication preferences by refraining from making overbearing or invasive follow-up attempts that could come across as aggressive or desperate.

Patience: Recognize that hiring processes can vary in length and complexity, so be patient and resilient while you wait for updates or responses from interviews.

Professional Networking

This requires job seekers to connect through LinkedIn, networking events, and informational interviews with recruiters or recruitment agencies.

LinkedIn connection: Job seekers should thank interviewers and hiring managers for the chance to connect and remain informed about pertinent announcements and updates by sending them a personalized LinkedIn connection request.

Networking events: In order to grow professional networks, job seekers must forge new connections and stay up-to-date on job openings and industry trends by attending conferences, workshops, or industry events.

Informational interviews: Job seekers should arrange for informational interviews with experts in the sector of their chosen specialty to get suggestions, counsel, and connections for furthering their career development.

Thank-you notes following interviews have a good impact on interviewers' opinions of job seekers' professionalism, zeal, and interpersonal skills (Lu and Dillahunt 2021). Thank-you notes raise the possibility of employment offers. In another study, Miller (2022) mentions the value of professional networking and relationship-building for career advancement and the success of job searches. The study also highlights the benefits of keeping in touch with interviewers and business professionals about potential future opportunities and joint ventures.

7.6. Building Relationships with Recruitment Agencies

This section provides an understanding of four areas: networking strategies and platforms, maintaining professional online profiles and presence, engaging with recruitment consultants and advisors, and seeking and providing constructive feedback.

A. Effective Networking Strategies and Platforms

Using several platforms to engage with recruiters, business professionals, and possible employers is essential to developing relationships with recruitment agencies. It is also important to use engaging networking methods. Successful networking increases awareness, broadens professional ties, and facilitates access to employment prospects.

Attending Professional Networking Events

Attending professional networking events like industry and business conferences and networking mixers is important because it can help expand one's professional cycle and create new opportunities. Job seekers should attend industry-specific conferences, seminars, and workshops to connect with hiring managers, recruiters, and industry leaders. These events provide opportunities to exchange ideas and stay informed about the latest trends and advancements. Additionally, networking mixers, such as career fairs and meet-and-greet events hosted by recruitment agencies and professional associations, offer valuable chances to expand their network and explore potential career opportunities.

Online Networking Platforms

Online networking platforms provide a virtual space for individuals to connect, communicate, and collaborate with others over the Internet. To increase image visibility, job seekers should create and optimize professional profiles on online platforms such as LinkedIn, X, Facebook, and Instagram. Through these online platforms, job seekers should showcase their experiences, talents, and accomplishments. Job seekers can also connect with peers, recruiters, and community groups, as well as join online professional associations and forums. To increase their visibility and network, job seekers should engage with and contribute to online discussion boards and community groups in their areas of interest. Find like-minded people or peers and exchange ideas.

Alumni Networks

Job seekers should be part of their alumni associations and networks of educational institutions to engage with their colleagues and gain access to job opportunities while making use of the alumni resources for career help and mentorship. Also, job seekers should endeavor to attend alumni meetings, events, celebrations, and reunions to reconnect with old classmates, build relationships, and explore opportunities.

Informational Interviews

Job seekers should reach out to referrals, networking contacts, and industry professionals for informational interviews to get suggestions, guidance, and advice on navigating the job market, forming connections, and pursuing career pathways. To obtain individualized support, constructive criticism, and chances for career advancement, job seekers should look for mentorship and advice from seasoned professionals in their areas of work interest.

Social Media Engagement

One of the largest platforms to gain industry insight is X, formerly called Twitter. Job seekers should actively participate in X chats, industry-specific hashtags, and online forums to engage with recruiters, thought leaders, and industry influencers. By contributing insights on topics relevant to their careers, job seekers can increase their visibility. Additionally, Facebook, with over a billion daily visits, remains a larger platform that offers valuable networking opportunities. Here, job seekers should have a reputable profile on Facebook, network with colleagues, exchange resources, and get updates about job openings. Job seekers should actively participate in groups, pages, and communities focused on professional growth, job opportunities, and industry debates.

Buettner (2017) mentions that professional networking activities, both online and offline, have a positive influence on career progression, pay negotiation, and access to job prospects during the job search process. Haidar and Keune (2021) and Gandini (2016) found that those who actively participate in networking activities, such as professional events, interacting on online forums, and requesting informational interviews, report better job satisfaction and career success. Furthermore, Levine (2015) mentions the value of networking in fostering professional relationships and accessing career opportunities by highlighting the role of networking in providing social support, information sharing, and career advancement.

B. Maintaining Professional Online Profiles and Presence

A well-established professional presence and online profile are important for building contacts with recruitment agencies, attracting new employers, and effectively exhibiting your skills, experiences, and accomplishments. Therefore, optimizing online profiles, interacting with pertinent material, and controlling digital reputation are all part of maintaining a professional online presence. Here are several ways one can maintain a professional online profile and presence:

LinkedIn Profile Optimization

Ensure the profile includes the job seeker's complete and thorough professional background, summary, work experience, educational qualifications, skills, and relevant certifications. Recruiters can gain a comprehensive overview of a job seeker's professional background and experience. Job seekers should also use keyword optimization to enhance their visibility and searchability by recruiters and employers. This involves incorporating relevant keywords, skills, and industry-specific terms into their LinkedIn profile, summary, headline, and skills section. Additionally, optimizing a LinkedIn profile includes customizing the profile banner, picture, and background to reflect the job seeker's personal brand, values, and professional interests. This way, job seekers can establish a visually appealing and cohesive online presence.

Online Portfolio Development

Job seekers should create their personal website or online portfolio to showcase their accomplishments, projects, work samples, and client endorsements. This will provide more background information and proof of their competencies. Incorporate visual content on the website to showcase the job seekers' creativity, storytelling abilities, and attention to detail. Examples of visual content include photos, videos, and infographics.

Creating and Distributing Content

In order to establish yourself as a subject matter expert and thought leader in your field, publish unique articles, blog posts, or thought leadership pieces on LinkedIn Pulse. Through articles, publications, and writings, job seekers can share their knowledge, experience, and industry views. Make use of your LinkedIn feed to actively communicate with others, share knowledge, and show that you are aware of current events and trends in the field by posting pertinent articles, news updates, and industry insights.

Online Professionalism and Privacy

To maintain a balance between visibility and privacy, job seekers should review and modify their social media platform's privacy settings to manage who can see their profile, connections, and activities. Also, job seekers need to be discreet and professional in all their interactions, posts, and comments. Steer clear of contentious issues and conduct that could damage their industry's reputation.

Online Endorsements and Recommendations

On LinkedIn, job seekers can receive skill endorsements when they request them and offer them to friends. It is a great way to validate competence and boost credibility in specific fields of interest. Also, job seekers can highlight their strengths, accomplishments, and contributions to previous work roles or projects by asking for recommendations and testimonials from coworkers, managers, or clients.

Having a strong online presence and profile can significantly increase the likelihood of catching the attention of recruiters. It can also provide job seekers with interview invitations and job offers. Hosain and Mamun (2023) highlight the importance of optimized and comprehensive LinkedIn accounts by stating that users are more likely to get employment through the site if their profiles are complete. Furthermore, Krings et al. (2021) highlight the impact of online recommendations and endorsements on the perceived credibility and trustworthiness of recruiters' views and decisions during candidates' evaluation and selection processes.

C. Engaging with Recruitment Consultants and Advisers

Effective engagement with recruitment consultants and advisers requires relationship building, effective communication, and collaboration to access job prospects and receive individualized career guidance. Interacting with recruiters expands networks, improves exposure, and facilitates access to employment openings.

Proactive Outreach

Job seekers should engage in proactive outreaches by attending job fairs, industry conferences, and events organized by recruitment agencies to network, meet recruiters, and indicate interest in learning more about possible career pathways and job opportunities. Also, job seekers should send out cold outreaches through emails, LinkedIn, or professional networking sites. The email should contain a self-introduction, discussions on career objectives, and requests for information about relevant job opportunities or services offered.

Informational Interviews

Job seekers should arrange consultation sessions or informational interviews with recruitment consultants to talk about preferences, experiences, talents, and professional goals. Job seekers can also inquire about personalized advice and suggestions regarding job search strategies and opportunities. Another important component requires job seekers to have market insights. In order to match job search efforts with employer preferences and market realities, it is necessary for job seekers to get updates and insights from recruitment consultants on industry demands, upcoming opportunities, and current employment market trends.

A Review of the Résumé and Profile

Job seekers should be open to criticism of their résumés. As a result, job seekers should seek feedback and revisions on their résumés to ensure that their résumé, LinkedIn profile, and online portfolio align with industry standards, maximize visibility, and appeal to employers. Additionally, collaborating with recruitment consultants can help enhance these profiles. By doing so, job seekers can achieve effective professional branding, positioning, and messaging, allowing them to stand out from the competition and clearly convey their unique selling point.

Matching Job Seekers with Suitable Job Opportunities and Providing Referrals

There is a need to make use of the knowledge and connections of recruitment consultants to gain access to exclusive and hidden job opportunities. Job seekers should seek tailored job recommendations and referrals based on interests, experiences, competencies, and career goals. Similarly, job seekers should work with recruitment consultants to represent them as candidates, negotiate offers, and interact with potential employers during the recruitment process.

Professional Development

Professional development is a significant aspect for anyone seeking to improve their career prospects. Recruitment consultants should actively pursue professional development to enhance their skills, obtain certifications, stay competitive in the job market, and foster professional growth. There is a need to work collaboratively with recruitment consultants to create a personalized career development plan, set achievable goals, and identify areas of improvement and growth opportunities that fit one's interests, strengths, and ambitions.

Boswell, Payne, and Bowman (2024) mention that candidates who actively communicate with recruitment consultants are more likely than passive candidates to acquire job opportunities, invitations to interviews, and receive offers of employment. Ling et al. (2018) highlight that job seekers who received individualized career counseling and coaching from recruitment consultants reported greater levels of work satisfaction, career clarity, and professional advancement. Furthermore, Lu and colleagues (2022) express the importance of recruitment consultants in helping job seekers through difficult times of unemployment or career changes by offering them emotional support, motivation, and encouragement.

D. Seeking and Delivering Constructive Feedback

Building positive relationships with recruitment agencies, encouraging mutual understanding, and supporting ongoing process development all depend on the effective delivery of constructive feedback. Requesting and offering feedback can help recruiters and applicants alike by improving expectations, alignment, accountability, and openness.

Candidate Feedback

Job seekers need interview briefs because they allow them to get insight into their performance, areas of strength and growth requirements, and general fit for the role and organization by asking recruitment firms for comments after job interviews. Furthermore, job seekers can identify areas for improvement, optimization, and alignment with employer preferences and expectations by soliciting feedback on cover letters, résumés, and other application materials in order to help recruitment agencies improve their services and procedures, provide feedback on your general impressions of them, including communication, responsiveness, and professionalism.

Agency Feedback

To assist in informed decision-making, alignment with client needs, and ongoing improvement in the candidate selection processes, there is a need to provide recruitment agencies with feedback on candidates' qualifications, experiences, and appropriateness for certain roles. Additionally, job seekers should provide feedback on recruiters' recruitment and selection processes, timelines, and communication strategies. Recruitment agencies can use this feedback to identify areas for improvement, enhance efficiency, and optimize the candidate experience. To ensure that agencies meet expectations, address concerns, and maintain a positive working relationship, job seekers should share their thoughts on the professionalism, responsiveness, and quality of services.

Feedback Channels

Job seekers can engage with recruitment agencies through structured questionnaires, feedback meetings, and online platforms. Job seekers can participate in structured feedback questionnaires designed by recruitment agencies to provide detailed input on a range of topics related to the hiring process, such as candidate experience, communication, and service quality. Through feedback meetings or discussions with recruitment consultants, recruitment agencies can get feedback on recommendations for process improvement, relationship building, and enhancing services. Recruitment agencies can utilize online platforms to promote accountability and transparency. Also, review sites or testimonials can help job seekers share their experiences and opinions about the professionalism, efficacy, and services provided by recruitment firms.

Constructive Criticism

Constructive criticisms should be detail-oriented, balanced, and professional. Job seekers who are detail-oriented can avoid giving generalized or ambiguous criticism that could be counterproductive or demoralizing. Job seekers should provide clear, actionable feedback that is relevant, constructive, and focused on behaviors, outcomes, or areas for growth. They should strike a healthy balance by acknowledging their achievements, strengths, and areas of excellence, while also highlighting opportunities for further development and improvement. Job seekers should express criticism in a courteous, sympathetic, and professional manner, highlighting a team-based strategy for ongoing development and shared successes.

Continuous Improvement

In order to address identified areas for development and increase overall effectiveness, there is a need to incorporate input from applicants and recruiting agencies into ongoing initiatives for process improvement, service upgrades, and training programs. Furthermore, to encourage openness, confidence, and continual development in the hiring process, create iterative feedback loops and systems for continuing interactions, discussions, and cooperation between hiring organizations, recruitment agencies, and job seekers.

Research indicates a connection between feedback-seeking behaviors and superior job performance, learning orientation, and career advancement. Studies by Gara and LaPorte (2020) and Liu, Huang, and Wang (2014) show that environments rich in feedback and marked by accountability, open communication, and transparency encourage cooperation and creativity among stakeholders in the hiring process. Also, feedback can help people become more effective, both personally and professionally, foster self-awareness, and encourage ongoing performance and result improvement.

7.7. Negotiating Job Offers and Contracts

This section provides an in-depth exploration of how job seekers and employers negotiate job offers and contracts. Topics will focus on evaluating compensation packages and benefits, negotiation techniques and strategies, understanding legal and contractual obligations, resolving disputes, and managing expectations. A. Evaluating compensation packages and benefits

The negotiation of employment offers and contracts is a crucial phase in the recruitment process, during which job seekers evaluate and discuss remuneration packages and benefits provided by employers. This section examines the elements that are considered when assessing compensation packages and benefits, emphasizing the importance of making decisions based on evidence and the role of negotiation in reaching agreements that are advantageous for all parties concerned.

Evaluating Compensation Packages

The compensation packages discussed here are base salary, variable compensation, and benefits packages.

The Base Salary

Employers allocate the base salary as the fundamental component of a compensation package, representing its monetary worth. Job seekers should assess the base compensation by considering industry benchmarks and market rates, as well as their expertise, experience, and qualifications. By utilizing online tools and industry statistics, job seekers can assess a job offer's competitiveness by researching compensation benchmarks and conducting salary comparisons using online tools and industry statistics.

Variable Compensation

Aside from the fixed income, job seekers should also take into account variable remuneration elements, such as bonuses, commissions, and profit-sharing agreements. Variable remuneration offers the chance for rewards and incentives based on performance, ensuring that the job seeker's financial interests are in line with the organization's goals and performance measures. To comprehend the entire earning potential, job seekers must evaluate the structure, eligibility requirements, and possible payout of variable compensation.

Benefit Packages

Employers frequently provide a variety of benefits to make remuneration packages more appealing and promote the well-being of their employees. Job seekers should thoroughly evaluate the advantages offered, such as medical coverage, pension schemes, allocated vacation time, adaptable work schedules, and prospects for career growth. An assessment of the extent, worth, and pertinence of advantages to personal requirements and preferences can guide the process of making decisions and formulating negotiation strategies. The SHRM (2021) employee benefits report indicates that the majority of organizations provide health care benefits (88 percent), retirement savings plans (77 percent), paid time off (76 percent), and flexible work arrangements (58 percent). Also, Glassdoor (2021) found that the majority of employees, specifically 80 percent, prioritize health insurance as the most significant benefit when assessing job offers. Retirement plans rank second, with 61 percent of employees considering them crucial, followed by paid time off at 58 percent.

Negotiation Strategies

Employing effective negotiating strategies can help job seekers optimize their income and benefits, all while fostering constructive connections with employers. Job seekers should:

Conduct research and gather data on industry norms, market trends, and competitor strategies to strengthen negotiating arguments and provide evidence for requesting better salaries and benefits.

Direct attention toward value by prioritizing the importance and contributions that individuals offer to the organization, accentuating pertinent skills, experiences, and accomplishments that warrant increased salary and benefits.

Establish priority interests by determining the most important aspects to consider in compensation negotiations while emphasizing key areas, such as salary, benefits, professional advancement prospects, and maintaining a healthy work-life balance.

Uphold professionalism by engaging in negotiations with professionalism, openness, and honesty with the aim of producing mutually advantageous agreements that satisfy the interests of both sides.

In summary, assessing the remuneration packages and benefits is an important component of negotiating job offers and contracts. Job seekers should evaluate the base pay, variable compensation, and benefits package offered by a company in comparison to the standards of the industry, personal preferences, and how well they align with the organization. Job seekers can improve wage packages and secure favorable employment agreements by using evidence-based decision-making and effective negotiation strategies. This approach leads to mutually beneficial outcomes for both job seekers and employers, promoting long-term satisfaction and success in the workplace.

B. Negotiation Techniques and Strategies

Candidates should utilize effective techniques and strategies to negotiate employment offers and contracts in order to achieve good outcomes while also keeping positive connections with organizations. This section examines negotiation techniques and strategies that applicants might employ to navigate the negotiation process effectively.

Negotiation Techniques

The negotiation techniques recognized are preparation, active listening, assertiveness, and flexibility.

Preparation

Successful negotiation starts with comprehensive and effective preparation. Prospective job seekers must conduct a thorough study of industry standards, market trends, and organizational practices in order to set practical expectations and determine key negotiation priorities. Acquiring data on wage benchmarks, benefits packages, and similar job offers enables candidates to make well-informed choices and put forth persuasive arguments during negotiations. The International Journal of Management Reviews (2021) shows that the level of preparation in negotiation has a significant impact on the outcomes. Well-prepared negotiators tend to secure more favorable agreements compared to those who are unprepared.

Active listening

Active listening is a fundamental negotiation skill that enables job seekers to understand the needs, interests, and concerns of both parties. By listening attentively to the employer's perspective, candidates can identify common ground, clarify misunderstandings, and explore mutually beneficial solutions. Demonstrating empathy and respect fosters trust and rapport. It also paves the way for constructive dialogue and agreement.

Assertiveness

Assertiveness entails confidently and clearly arguing for one's own interests and preferences while still showing respect for the interests of the other party. Job seekers should confidently and effectively articulate their unique selling points, highlighting their expertise, past achievements, and the positive impact they can make on the organization. Assertiveness enables job seekers to effectively communicate their demands and preferences in a confident and self-assured manner while upholding professionalism and showing respect. Harvard Business Review (HBR) (2020) found that successful negotiation involves a combination of assertiveness and empathy. Effective negotiators can assert their own interests while also actively listening to the opposing party's point of view.

Flexibility

Flexibility is an important aspect of negotiation because it allows job seekers to adjust to evolving situations, explore different options, and reach innovative agreements. Job seekers should be receptive to examining various negotiating outcomes and contemplating concessions in order to achieve mutually agreeable agreements. Flexibility showcases a readiness to cooperate and discover mutually beneficial resolutions that satisfy the requirements of both parties.

Negotiation Strategies

The negotiation strategies discussed in this sub-section are the Best Alternative to a Negotiated Agreement (BATNA), framing, collaborative problem-solving, and assertive closing.

BATNA

The BATNA strategy entails the identification of alternative choices and potential outcomes in the event that discussions do not result in a mutually acceptable agreement. Job seekers should analyze their BATNA and utilize it as a standard to measure the attractiveness of prospective offers and guide their negotiating choices. Having a robust BATNA enables candidates to negotiate with authority and assurance.

Framing

Deliberately manipulating the negotiating discourse and the way issues are perceived helps achieve favorable conclusions. Job seekers have the ability to present their negotiation arguments and offers positively, highlighting the advantages, benefits, and compatibility with the goals of the company. Framing strategies allow job seekers to exert influence over the narrative and steer conversations toward predetermined objectives.

Collaborative Problem-Solving

Collaborative problem-solving promotes cooperation among parties to tackle common difficulties and attain mutually advantageous results. Job seekers should embrace a cooperative approach, prioritizing mutual interests, collective objectives, and innovative resolutions that optimize value for all parties involved. Collaboration promotes trust, strengthens relationships, and results in long-lasting agreements.

Assertive Closing

Assertive closing boldly and decisively ends discussions after agreement terms have been established. Prospective job seekers are required to provide a concise overview of the main ideas, verify the specifics of the agreement, and develop unambiguous plans and deadlines for carrying out the agreed-upon actions. By employing an assertive closing, one can strengthen their dedication to the mutually agreed-upon arrangement and guarantee both transparency and responsibility in the future.

Prospective job seekers must utilize effective approaches and strategies to attain good outcomes when negotiating employment offers and contracts. Job seekers can achieve successful negotiation outcomes and create mutually beneficial agreements by thoroughly preparing, practicing active listening, assertively advocating for their interests, and remaining flexible throughout the process. Negotiation techniques such as evaluating BATNA, framing, collaborative problem-solving, and aggressive closure improve negotiation success and lead to favorable results for both job seekers and employers.

C. Understanding Legal and Contractual Obligations

Having a comprehensive understanding of legal and contractual duties is of utmost importance for both job seekers and employers when engaging in the negotiation process of employment offers and contracts. This section explores the legal and contractual factors that need to be taken into account, highlighting the importance of adherence, precision, and safeguarding rights.

Legal Obligations

The legal obligations include the following:

Employment Laws and Regulations

The SHRM (2021) emphasized the importance of adhering to employment rules. According to the SHRM study, 92 percent of organizations actively implement steps to maintain compliance with employment legislation at the federal, state, and local levels. Job seekers and employers need to have relevant knowledge of the employment rules and regulations that govern job relationships. These may encompass legislation pertaining to the minimum wage, compensation for working beyond regular hours, measures against unfair treatment, ensuring a safe work environment, and protecting the rights of employees. Complying with legal standards guarantees adherence to and protection of the rights of all parties.

Contractual Agreement

Employment contracts define the specifics of employment (terms and conditions). It also encompasses job duties and responsibilities, remuneration, benefits, termination protocols, and nondisclosure provisions. Prospective job seekers should thoroughly examine the provisions of a contract to verify that they are clear, equitable, and in line with their expectations and entitlements. Having a clear and robust comprehension of contractual obligations reduces uncertainty and limits the risk of conflict. The US Department of Labor (DOL) and the Fair Labor Standards Act (FLSA) establish regulations for minimum wages, overtime, documentation and record-keeping, and restrictions on the employment of minors. These regulations apply to both full-time and part-time employees in the private and public sectors across federal, state, and local government entities.

Contractual Obligations

These include the following:

Terms and Conditions

Prospective candidates should carefully review employment agreements to gain a comprehensive understanding of their employment terms and conditions. This includes areas such as job title, responsibilities, working hours, remuneration arrangement, benefits, probationary period, and provisions related to termination. Precise and unambiguous contractual language aids in avoiding misinterpretations and promotes efficient communication among the involved parties. The International Journal of Human Resource Management (IJHRM) conducted a study in 2021 that found that noncompete agreements are becoming more prevalent in employment contracts. Specifically, 40 percent of firms now mandate employees to sign noncompete clauses as a prerequisite for employment.

Confidentiality and Noncompete Clauses

Deloitte's survey in 2020 found that 61 percent of firms include confidentiality terms in their employment contracts to safeguard sensitive information and ensure data privacy. Employment contracts may include confidentiality and noncompete clauses to protect the employer's interests, sensitive information, and intellectual property.

Candidates should carefully evaluate the scope, duration, and enforceability of these clauses to avoid overly restricting their future job prospects or rights.

Compliance and Due Diligence

Here, discussions are centered on legal consultations and due diligence.

Legal Consultation

Prior to receiving a job offer, candidates may obtain legal counsel or consultation to examine employment agreements, clarify legal entitlements and responsibilities, and resolve any worries or uncertainties. Legal professionals possess the ability to offer valuable perspectives, detect any hazards, and provide advice on negotiation strategies in order to safeguard the interests of candidates. The American Bar Association (ABA) (2021) highlights the importance of seeking legal advice during employment contract negotiations. According to the study, a significant 79 percent of surveyed attorneys strongly recommend engaging in a legal review of employment contracts in order to protect their client's interests.

Due Diligence

Employers must ensure that employment contracts adhere to relevant laws and regulations and do not include clauses that infringe upon employee rights or legal norms. Performing thorough research and analysis while creating and examining contracts reduces the chances of legal liabilities, improves clarity, and promotes confidence and reliance between the involved parties. LexisNexis (2020) study poll found that 67 percent of organizations perform legal due diligence during employment contract discussions. Organizations perform legal due diligence during employment contract discussions to identify and mitigate legal risks stemming from the contract's terms and conditions.

In summary, both candidates and employers need to have a clear understanding of their legal and contractual obligations when negotiating job offers and contracts. Complying with employment rules and regulations, examining contract terms and conditions, and getting legal advice as needed ensure adherence, transparency, and rights protection by giving top priority to adhering to legal requirements, ensuring openness, and conducting thorough investigations. These parties can create employment contracts that are just and advantageous, promoting trust, responsibility, and adherence to legal norms.

D. Resolving Disputes and Managing Expectations

Resolving conflicts and effectively handling expectations are important components of negotiating employment offers and contracts. In this section, an examination of efficient approaches for resolving problems, overseeing expectations, and upholding favorable connections is explored between job seekers and employers.

Resolving Disputes

Disputes are resolved through open communication, mediation, and arbitration. We provide the explanation as follows:

Open Communication

The Society for Human Resource Management (SHRM) (2021) study found that implementing open communication and conflict resolution training are successful methods for reducing workplace conflicts. Potential job seekers and employers need to have a conducive environment that encourages the free discussion and resolution of concerns and grievances. The root causes of conflicts can be identified through the encouragement of open dialogue, attentive listening, and empathy, which promotes common understanding. According to SHRM (2021), 82 percent of organizations surveyed reported offering conflict resolution training to their employees.

Mediation and Arbitration

When it becomes impossible to resolve disputes and conflicts through direct negotiation, mediation, and arbitration are the alternative methods to resolve disputes. Meditation is the process where an impartial third party helps facilitate negotiations between different parties in order to achieve a settlement that is agreeable to all. Arbitration, on the other hand, resolves conflicts by presenting them to an impartial arbitrator who makes a final and enforceable decision based on facts and legal principles. According to a study by the American Arbitration Association (AAA) (2021), mediation and arbitration are commonly employed in employment disputes. Approximately 57 percent of organizations have incorporated arbitration clauses into their employment contracts as a means to efficiently and cost-effectively resolve disputes.

Managing Expectations

In managing expectations, it is important to set clear and realistic expectations, written agreements, and conflict resolution strategies.

Clear Expectations

It is important to establish clear and attainable expectations from the outset to avert future misunderstandings and disputes. During the negotiation process, job seekers and employers need to engage in discussions regarding employment responsibilities, performance expectations, goals, and objectives. Reaching a shared understanding of important terms and conditions helps to synchronize and decrease the chances of not meeting expectations. In 2021, Glassdoor conducted a survey revealing that 88 percent of employees consider their employer's establishment of explicit expectations important for their job satisfaction and performance.

Written Agreements

Recording mutually agreed-upon terms and conditions in written contracts serves as a point of reference for effectively managing expectations and settling conflicts. Employment contracts should clearly and precisely specify the tasks and responsibilities of the job, the amount and type of payment, the perks and advantages, the criteria for evaluating performance, and the procedures for ending the contract, using language that leaves no room for confusion or misinterpretation. Written contracts establish a structure for holding individuals responsible and guarantee that both parties have a clear comprehension of their entitlements and responsibilities. According to *Forbes* (2020), written contacts significantly reduce the probability of conflicts and legal actions. A notable 70 percent of legal experts suggest utilizing written agreements to clearly define rights and responsibilities and avoid any misinterpretations.

Effective Conflict Resolution Strategies

Two strategies are explored here: collaboration in problem-solving and compromise and flexibility.

Collaborative Problem-Solving

Collaborative problem-solving entails the joint effort of both job seekers and employers to identify underlying problems, explore various solutions, and ultimately come to mutually agreeable resolutions. Job seekers and employers should prioritize mutual interests, aligned objectives, and mutually beneficial outcomes that cater to the needs of both sides. A 2021 study published in the Harvard Negotiation Law Review demonstrated that collaborative problem-solving and compromise are effective conflict-resolution strategies. The study found that 75 percent of negotiators successfully resolved disputes using these approaches.

Compromise and Flexibility

Compromise and flexibility are important for reaching a consensus and accommodating a wide range of viewpoints and interests. Both job seekers and employers should demonstrate a willingness to compromise and adapt their stances in order to achieve mutually agreeable outcomes. Flexibility exemplifies a dedication to discovering resolutions that adequately address the requirements of all parties involved. The *Journal of Applied Psychology* (2020) conducted a study that indicates flexibility and adaptability are crucial qualities for effective negotiators. These skills allow negotiators to effectively negotiate intricate negotiations and discover innovative resolutions to conflicts.

Bear in mind that the process of resolving conflicts and effectively handling expectations are important aspects of negotiating employment offers and contracts. Effective communication, mediation, and arbitration aid in resolving conflicts while establishing clear expectations, utilizing formal agreements, and employing collaborative problem-solving strategies to assist in managing expectations and avoiding misunderstandings. Through the implementation of efficient conflict resolution techniques, candidates and employers can effectively negotiate negotiations, maintain relationships, and achieve mutually agreeable results by implementing efficient conflict resolution techniques.

7.8. Managing Expectations and Career Development

A. Setting Realistic Career Goals and Objectives

Setting realistic and attainable career goals and objectives is important for successful career planning and advancement. In this section, discussions are centered on the importance, strategies, and impact of setting realistic career goals and objectives to achieve career success and satisfaction.

The Importance of Achieving Career Goals and Objectives

The importance of attaining career goals and objectives is as follows:

Direction and focus: Having a realistic career goal helps job seekers establish a clear path and concentration in their professional pursuits.

Job seekers can focus their energy and resources on meaningful endeavors that align with their personal ambitions by setting achievable goals.

Motivation and persistence: Setting realistic career objectives acts as a catalyst for job seekers to stay motivated and determined in their pursuit of their desires. Achieving career objectives cultivates a feeling of achievement and advancement. It inspires job seekers to surmount obstacles and persist in their professional aspirations.

Measurement of progress: Setting realistic career objectives allows job seekers to monitor their advancement and assess their accomplishments over a period of time. Through the establishment of quantifiable goals, individuals may evaluate their progress, identify areas for improvement, and adapt their strategies accordingly to remain on track toward their intended results.

Strategies for Setting Realistic Career Goals

The strategies discussed here include SMART, self-assessment, research, and planning.

SMART goals: SMART stands for specific, measurable, achievable, relevant, and time-bound. It is a widely recognized and accepted method for establishing realistic career objectives. In order to promote clarity, accountability, and achievability in the goal-setting process, job seekers must ensure that their goals are set using the SMART framework.

Self-assessment: This involves conducting exercises to discover one's strengths, limitations, interests, and values, which can provide valuable information for developing goals. By connecting one's job goals with their personal qualities and desires, individuals can establish objectives that are in harmony with their innate aspirations. Studies (Busque, Ratelle, and Le Corff 2022; Bayona, Caballer, and Peiro 2020) mention that aligning career goals with personal values and interests can lead to job satisfaction and high performance.

Research and planning: Conducting research and planning is important in order to gather information about industry trends, job market demands, and skill requirements. This is necessary to establish realistic career goals. Engaging in market research and strategic planning allows job seekers to discern prospects for expansion, foresee obstacles, and synchronize their objectives with evolving patterns in their selected fields of interest.

In summary, establishing realistic career goals and objectives is important because of the guidance it provides for job seekers in terms of career advancement and achievements. In order to promote motivation, focus, and progress in professional advancement, job seekers should set realistic goals. Job seekers can set realistic goals by using SMART criteria and aligning their aspirations with personal values and industry trends. Effective goal-setting strategies enable job seekers to navigate their careers with confidence and purpose, leading to greater satisfaction and fulfillment in their chosen professions.

B. Pursuing Continuous Learning and Development Opportunities

Continuous learning and development are integral to career growth and professional development. In this section, the importance of continuous learning is identified and discussed. Also discussed are the strategies for pursuing continuous learning and the impact of lifelong learning on career progression. There is a positive relationship between continuous learning and career progression (Sugiarti 2022). Job seekers who actively participate in continuous skill development and educational programs tend to have greater job satisfaction, performance, and promotability in comparison to those who do not prioritize continuous learning.

The Importance of Continuous Learning and Development

The importance of continuous learning and development is discussed as follows:

Continuous learning enhances adaptability and resilience. Hence, it enables job seekers to acquire the necessary information and skills to adjust to changing job demands, technological progress, and industry developments. To maintain resilience and adaptability in the face of workplace changes, job seekers should stay updated on emerging trends.

Competitive advantage: Continuous engagement in learning improves job seekers' skills, knowledge, and market value in their specific areas of competence. Through the acquisition of new skills, certifications, and qualifications job seekers can distinguish themselves from their peers by acquiring new skills, certifications, and qualifications, allowing them to position themselves for career advancement and prospects.

Career growth and satisfaction: Continuous learning promotes both personal and professional development. It motivates and encourages job seekers to seek demanding positions, broaden their duties, and attain increased gratification in their jobs. Engaging in skill development and self-improvement enables job seekers to confidently and enthusiastically follow their passions and objectives.

Strategies for Pursuing Continuous Learning

There are several ways job seekers can engage in continuous learning. Examples of some of these ways are formal education, online learning, and on-the-job training.

Formal education: This involves enrolling in degree programs, certifications, workshops, and seminars given by educational institutions and professional organizations. This allows individuals to access structured learning opportunities that increase their skills and help them acquire knowledge. Formal education programs provide extensive course content, experienced teaching, and official certifications that verify job seekers' knowledge and skills in particular areas.

Online learning: Job seekers can conveniently access a diverse array of courses, tutorials, and resources specifically designed to cater to their unique learning requirements and preferences through online learning platforms like Coursera, Udemy, and LinkedIn Learning. Online learning systems allow individuals to learn at their own pace and convenience from any location with an internet connection, providing flexibility, convenience, and accessibility.

On-the-job training: On-the-job training is experiential in nature, so it requires job seekers to be active participants in on-the-job training programs, mentorship opportunities, and work rotations within organizations. These are practical ways job seekers and employees can gain hands-on experience and enhance their skills. It also allows employees to apply theoretical knowledge to real-world activities and receive valuable feedback and direction from seasoned experts. The Association for Talent Development (ATD) (2021) revealed that organizations that prioritize employee development and provide extensive learning opportunities experience higher levels of employee engagement, retention, and productivity. This demonstrates the significant impact of continuous learning initiatives on driving organizational success.

Engaging in continuous learning and seeking out opportunities for personal and professional growth is crucial for individuals to maintain a competitive edge, adapt to changing circumstances, and find satisfaction in their work. By committing to continuous learning, utilizing various educational resources, and dedicating time and effort to developing new skills, employees can enhance their knowledge and abilities. Also, continuous learning allows employees to progress in their professional lives and attain higher levels of fulfillment while continuously achieving in the changing work environment.

C. Adapting to Changes in the Job Market and Industry Trends

Job seekers and employees need to be adaptable to changes in order to stay relevant and competitive in their jobs. Adaptability and flexibility are high skills that every employee should have, given the constant changes in the work market and industry trends. This section discusses the importance of adapting to changes, strategies for keeping up with industry changes, and the influence of adaptive skills on career resilience and progression. Job seekers and employees who are adaptable tend to have higher levels of job satisfaction, performance, and career advancement compared to those who are less adaptable (Dale 2020). Also, the World Economic Forum mentions that adaptability is an important talent for workforce resilience and readiness in the face of future challenges and disruptions. This emphasizes the importance of adaptability in effectively managing uncertainty in the employment market.

The Importance of Adapting to Changes

These include the following:

Market relevance: The job market experiences continuous changes influenced by technological advancements, economic fluctuations, and societal changes. Those who proactively adjust to these changes can capitalize on emerging opportunities, surmount problems, and maintain their relevance in their careers.

Career resilience. Career resilience provides individuals with the necessary skills, knowledge, and mindset to traverse uncertainties and disruptions effectively. Resilient professionals possess the ability to adapt, create new ideas, and transform themselves in order to succeed in the face of shifting circumstances, allowing them to flourish in a changing market environment.

Professional growth. Embracing change exposes job seekers and employees to new experiences, perspectives, and challenges, thereby aiding in their development. Flexible employees are receptive to acquiring new knowledge, engaging in experimentation, and consistently enhancing their skills, which empowers them to broaden their abilities and achieve their utmost potential in their professional endeavors.

Strategies for Adapting to Changes

The strategies for adapting to changes include continuous learning, networking and information sharing, flexibility, and open-mindedness.

Continuous learning: Engaging in continuous learning programs allows professionals to stay informed about industry advancements, emerging technologies, and evolving best practices. Through the allocation of resources toward skill development and the acquisition of knowledge, employees can effectively adjust to evolving employment demands and strategically position themselves for potential new prospects.

Networking and information sharing: Establishing professional connections and maintaining contact with colleagues, mentors, and influential figures in the field promotes the interchange of information and expertise. Networking platforms, industry events, and online groups offer vital information on industry trends, employment market dynamics, and career prospects.

Flexibility and open-mindedness: Developing a mentality of flexibility and open-mindedness is important for adjusting to shifts in the job market and industry trends. By accepting diverse perspectives, exploring alternative career options, and embracing new challenges, job seekers and employees can maintain their adaptability and responsiveness in the face of changing circumstances.

Job seekers and employees need to adapt to changes in the labor market and industry trends in order to maintain their relevance, resilience, and career growth. Through the adoption of continuous learning, the development of professional networks, and the cultivation of flexibility and open-mindedness, job seekers and employees can effectively navigate uncertainties, grasp opportunities, and prosper in the face of changing market dynamics.

D. Evaluating Long-Term Career Prospects and Aspirations

Assessing the future potential of one's career and personal ambitions is crucial for job seekers and employees to make informed decisions about their professional paths and pursue opportunities that align with their long-term goals. This section explores the importance of evaluating future career opportunities, effective assessment strategies, and how long-term planning impacts career satisfaction and success. Job seekers and employees who actively engage in long-term career planning and goal setting are more likely to experience higher levels of career satisfaction, job engagement, and general well-being (Coetzee 2021) in comparison to those who do not engage in such proactive career planning.

The Importance of Evaluating Long-Term Career Prospects

These include the following:

Strategic planning: Evaluating the potential for long-term success in one's profession allows job seekers to participate in strategic planning and establish specific objectives actively. Through the analysis of future trends, industry projections, and personal aspirations, job seekers and employees can discern potential areas for advancement, foresee obstacles, and formulate strategic plans to achieve long-term career goals.

Career alignment: Assessing the long-term prospects of a career helps job seekers and employees guarantee that their career goals are in line with their personal beliefs, interests, and aspirations. By evaluating potential career paths and opportunities, job seekers and employees can make informed decisions that align with their intrinsic motivations, enhancing their overall satisfaction and fulfillment in their professional lives.

Strategies for Evaluating Long-Term Career Prospects

These include the following:

Self-reflection: Engaging in reflective practice will allow job seekers and employees to identify and appreciate their strengths, weaknesses, passions, and values, which are important when assessing long-term employment opportunities. Through a comprehensive awareness of their core competencies and preferences, job seekers and employees can evaluate potential career paths that are in alignment with their abilities and passions.

Market research: It is the systematic collection and analysis of data to get insights into industry trends, job market demands, and future projections. Through the examination of labor market data, industry studies, and economic forecasts, individuals can discern emerging opportunities, skill deficiencies, and areas of expansion in their desired sectors.

Evaluating long-term career potential and ambitions is important for job seekers and employees to make well-informed decisions about their professional growth and seek opportunities that are in line with their objectives and principles. Through reflective practice, performing thorough market analysis, and strategic planning, job seekers and employees can effectively steer their professional paths. Also, job seekers and employees can navigate their careers with assurance, adaptability, and intention, which leads to satisfaction and achievement in their selected and intended career sector.

Conclusion

In summary, this chapter has examined the requirements and expectations of recruitment agencies from job seekers. Some of the topics discussed include understanding agency expectations that require job seekers to have a comprehensive understanding of the specific criteria and preferences of recruitment agencies. For example, job seekers need to engage with recruitment agencies with professionalism, qualifications, competencies, skills, adaptability, and sound industry knowledge. Another topic was the need for job seekers to acknowledge the services offered by recruitment agencies. These services include candidate sourcing, screening, interview preparation, and providing support during negotiations. Also, the recruitment industry is undergoing important evolutions driven by technological advancements, diversity and inclusion initiatives, and the growing prevalence of remote work. These forces are changing traditional recruitment strategies and approaches.

Practical recommendations for job seekers based on the knowledge acquired in this chapter are as follows:

Research and preparation: Prior to dealing with recruitment agencies, it is important to conduct comprehensive research to gain a clear grasp of areas of expertise, the consumer base, and expectations.

Professionalism and communication: It is important to have a professional attitude when dealing with recruitment agencies. This includes being punctual in your communication, meeting deadlines, and treating others with respect.

Continuous learning: Engaging and investing in continuous learning and skill development makes job seekers and employees relevant and desirable in the job market. It also improves their visibility and marketability in the job market.

Networking and relationship building: It is important to establish and cultivate professional relationships with recruitment consultants and industry contacts to broaden one's network and gain access to undisclosed career opportunities.

Adaptability and flexibility: These are important skills to have in every career endeavor. It is important to remain open-minded and willing to adjust to changes in the job market. Additionally, it is important to seize opportunities for personal and professional growth and advancement.

In the future, various trends will have a significant impact on recruitment processes and practices. Some of these trends include the following:

Technological integration: The use of AI, data analytics, and automation tools will completely transform recruitment processes. Therefore, technological transformation will drive recruitment agencies to become faster, more efficient, and more effective in candidate sourcing and screening.

Remote work: The increasing prevalence of remote work arrangements will require adaptations in recruitment practices because virtual recruitment processes are becoming more common, and flexible work is gaining more acceptance.

Diversity and inclusion: Recruitment strategies will increasingly focus on diversity and inclusion as organizations prioritize the recruitment of varied people and adopt inclusive recruiting strategies to promote innovation and achieve business success.

Skills-based hiring: Employers will prioritize skills and competencies over traditional qualifications when hiring, resulting in a trend towards skills-based tests and alternative credentialing methods.

In conclusion, the relationship between recruitment agencies and job seekers is multifaceted, as both parties have a reciprocal impact on each other's experiences and results in the job market. To improve competitiveness and boost the likelihood of finding rewarding job opportunities, job seekers should enhance their chances by comprehending and fulfilling the requirements of recruitment agencies. In order to successfully navigate professional pathways, job seekers must remain agile, proactive, and informed about emerging trends and practices in the evolving recruitment industry. Job seekers can strategically position themselves in the ever-evolving job market through a combination of research, preparation, professionalism, and adaptability.

Chapter 7:
Job Seekers Expectation from Recruitment Agencies

8.0. Introduction

Recruitment is a major process for organizations to recruit top talents to meet their staffing demands. This chapter provides an understanding of the importance of job seekers expectations from recruitment agencies. Multiple steps in the recruitment process include candidate sourcing, screening, selection, and onboarding. Employers employ a range of strategies to attract a pool of job seekers. The hiring process includes job advertisements, personal referrals, and recruitment agencies. The goal is to find skilled candidates who are qualified and align with the company's values. The main objective of this chapter is to explore job seekers' expectations from recruitment agencies by discussing the following topics: perspectives of job seekers and factors influencing job seekers' satisfaction. Through the discussions of these topics, the book hopes to help researchers, job seekers, and recruitment agencies improve outcomes, maximize recruitment practices, and enhance outcomes for all stakeholders.

8.1. The Job Seekers' Perspectives

This section discusses three main components, which include the reasons behind seeking assistance from recruitment agencies, expectations regarding services provided, and factors influencing job seekers' choice of recruitment agency.

Reasons for Seeking Assistance from Recruitment Agencies

Recruitment agencies are the middlemen between job seekers and hiring organizations; this makes these agencies integral to the job search process. Understanding why job seekers request assistance from recruitment agencies helps them to improve their services and ensure job seekers are more satisfied. Drawing from contemporary academic literature, this section examines the reasons behind the decisions of job seekers.

Reasons for Seeking Assistance

The reasons why job seekers seek assistance from recruitment agencies include the following:

Access to hidden opportunities: Obtaining access to unpublicized job openings is one of the main reasons why job seekers frequently use recruitment agencies. According to Davis and Aspray (2020), unofficial networks and recommendations fill a significant number of job openings. Recruitment agencies are an invaluable tool for accessing the underground labor market.

Expertise and guidance: There is a need for professional expertise and guidance during the job search process; hence, job seekers turn to recruitment agencies for help. Smith et al.'s (2019) study shows that recruitment agencies can improve job seekers' chances by offering expert advice on résumé writing, interview techniques, and career counseling.

Time efficiency: Job seekers often perceive that recruitment agencies can fasten the recruitment process and save them the time to fill out job applications. According to Jones and Johnson (2021), job seekers like how quickly recruitment agencies match their qualifications and skills with appropriate positions, saving them time on pointless application processes.

Recruitment agencies provide job seekers with networking and professional connection opportunities in their respective industrial sectors. Lee and Kim (2018) mention that recruitment agencies act as intermediaries between hiring organizations and job seekers, highlighting the value of networking in obtaining job referrals and expanding professional networks.

Increased market visibility: Working with recruiting firms can help job searchers become more visible in the labor market, especially among organizations that rely on them to find competent job seekers. Wang and Liu (2020) found that job seekers consider recruiting agencies as avenues to showcase their expertise, experience, and skills to a larger audience. The study further implies that job seekers perceive that being exposed to a larger audience helps improve their chances of landing a job.

Understanding these reasons for seeking assistance from recruitment agencies is important for recruitment agencies to properly customize their services and satisfy the needs of job seekers.

Expectations Regarding the Services Provided

Job seekers' expectations from recruitment agencies help determine their satisfaction and overall experience. This session delves into five specific expectations. **Personalized job matching**: Job seekers anticipate personalized job matching services from recruitment agencies that are based on their experience, qualifications, and desired career path. Personalized job recommendations based on personal interests and aspirations are important because they increase the likelihood of finding a positive fit for employment (Johnson and Smith 2021).

Communication transparency: This is another important expectation that job seekers have when working with recruitment agencies because it builds trust and confidence. Brown et al. (2019) mention that there is a need for recruitment agencies to be open and honest in their communication about job opportunities, salary negotiations, and other relevant details.

Timeliness and responsiveness: During the hiring process, job seekers anticipate that recruitment agencies will act promptly and responsively. Patel and Williams (2020) found that job seekers may become frustrated and dissatisfied with delays in contact or feedback, highlighting the significance of prompt interactions and updates from recruitment agencies.

Professional support and direction: Garcia and Martinez (2018) mention that job seekers want recruitment agencies that provide comprehensive support to improve their employability. Job seekers also appreciate comprehensive assistance in producing curriculum vitae, preparing for interviews, and career counseling.

Ethical and fair practices: Kim and Lee (2021) mention that job seekers expect recruitment agencies to maintain ethical standards in their dealings. Also, job seekers expect that the agencies work with integrity, confidentiality, and adherence to stipulated legal labor rules and regulations.

In order to meet these expectations, recruitment agencies must build rapport, increase service satisfaction, and gain the trust of seekers.

Factors influencing the choice of recruitment agencies

There are a number of factors that impact job seekers' views and preferences when it comes to deciding to work with a recruitment agency to get a job. This section delves into the primary factors that impact job seekers' selection or recruitment agencies.

Credibility and reputation: When choosing a recruitment firm, job seekers give careful thought to the agency's credibility and reputation. Smith and Johnson (2021) mention that job seekers are more likely to choose agencies that have the attributes of a solid industry presence, a track record of successful placements, and positive client testimonials. The reason is that these attributes give them confidence in the agency's ability to produce results.

Specialization and expertise: Job seekers give priority to recruitment agencies that have specialized knowledge of their desired industries or fields of interest. They believe that specialist agencies have better insights, networks, and awareness of specific job markers. According to Brown et al. (2020), working with specialized recruitment agencies increases the likelihood of finding relevant employment opportunities that fit with talents and career ambitions.

Range of services offered: Patel and Williams (2021) mention that job seekers value recruitment agencies that provide comprehensive services beyond simple job matching. Job seekers expect agencies to help with résumé writing, career counseling, and interview preparation. These extra services add to a more supportive and all-encompassing job search process.

Geographical coverage and reach: Lee and Kim (2019) suggest that job seekers prefer agencies with a broad network of hiring organizations and job opportunities spanning multiple states or cities. The geographical reach helps job seekers expand their options and increases the likelihood of finding suitable employment closer to their desired locations.

Cost and fee structure: c This helps job seekers make informed decisions that align with their preferences and financial budgets.

Recruitment agencies need to understand these factors so that they can effectively be positioned to attract potential organizations and meet the preferences and demands of job seekers.

8.2. Factors Influencing Job Seekers Satisfaction

Key factors affecting the job search experience also impact how satisfied job seekers are with recruitment agencies. This section covers four main factors: clear communication, quality job matches, quick responses, and support during the hiring process.

Communication and Transparency

Communication and transparency are important in order to determine how satisfied job seekers are with recruitment agencies. Communication and transparency are multifaceted when it comes to the recruitment process. Here, we explore the multifaceted nature of communication and transparency by exploring the following factors:

Components of Communication and Transparency

Clear and Timely Communication

Throughout the hiring process, job seekers appreciate recruitment agencies that keep the lines of communication open and concise. In order to keep job seekers informed and interested, Brown, Jones, and Miller (2021) found that clear explanations of the next steps, feedback from interviews, and frequent updates on the status of applications are important. Organizations that show professionalism and regard for job seekers' time and involvement in the process are those that communicate with promptness and consistency.

Accessibility and Responsiveness

Accessibility and responsiveness are essential components of effective communication that have an impact on job seekers' satisfaction. Smith and Johnson (2022) show that to satisfy the preferences of job seekers and promote smooth communication, recruitment agencies should be reachable by phone, email, or online platforms. Quick responses to questions, concerns, or requests for more information boost job seekers' trust in the organization's dedication to meeting their needs and promoting good relationships.

Transparency in Job Descriptions and Expectations

Transparency in job descriptions and expectations is important for managing the expectations of job seekers and facilitating the informed decision-making process. To match job seekers' goals with employer offers, it's important to share clear details about job roles, salaries, and benefits. Transparent agencies build trust, stronger relationships, and higher satisfaction with job seekers by earning their trust and credibility through their communication.

Feedback and Constructive Criticism

An important component of open communication that supports job seekers' development is providing constructive feedback and criticism. Even in situations where they may not be selected for a specific position, job seekers value organizations that provide feedback on their résumés, interview performance, and general candidacy (Brown et al. 2021). Positive feedback promotes a feeling of support and collaboration between job seekers and the agency. This is done by helping job seekers identify areas for improvement, refining job search strategies, and enhancing competitiveness in the job market.

Honesty and Integrity

These are the foundational principles of transparent communication. Patel and Williams (2022) mention that recruitment agencies should endeavor to be upright in their communication with job seekers. Moreover, agencies should be honest about any challenges or uncertainties during the hiring process. Employers appreciate agencies that communicate openly, uphold strong values and prioritize job seekers best interests, even when sharing bad news or setbacks. Cultural Sensitivity and Inclusion

To guarantee that job seekers from a variety of backgrounds feel appreciated, respected, and understood, communication must be inclusive and sensitive to cultural differences. According to Johnson and Martinez (2019), it's critical that employers communicate with job seekers in a way that is inclusive of all backgrounds, steer clear of stereotypes, and take into consideration cultural differences. Organizations that exhibit cultural competence and sensitivity provide a welcoming and inclusive atmosphere, thus increasing engagement and satisfaction.

The Quality of Job Matches

The quality of job matches that recruitment agencies institute impacts long-term engagement and success for job seekers. In this section, we explore the components of the quality of job matches inferred from academic literature.

Components of Quality of Matches

Alignment with Skills and Experiences

Job seekers give top priority to positions that closely match their professional experiences, skills, and qualifications. Smith and Johnson (2022) mention that job seekers value recruitment agencies that carefully evaluate their profiles and preferences in order to find positions that best utilize their skills and experience. A well-matched position improves job satisfaction and contributes to long-term job performance. It also helps job seekers advance in their careers because they are more likely to perform well in roles that make the most of their skills.

Fit with Career Aspirations

Brown et al. (2021) mention that it is important for recruitment agencies to understand job seekers' long-term professional goals in order to suggest job roles that present chances for advancement, development, and improvement. In order to create a sense of purpose and fulfillment in their professional journey, job seekers favor agencies that consider their career aspirations and offer opportunities that fit with their ambitions.

Cultural and Organizational Fit

Job seekers attach great value to job matches that offer a strong cultural and organizational fit. Employees give priority to positions in organizations whose values, mission, and workplace culture align with their personal preferences and beliefs (Garcia and Martinez, 2021). When connecting employees with employment openings, agencies that consider cultural fit along with skills and qualifications improve job seekers' satisfaction. These agencies also create a peaceful and comfortable work atmosphere that is consistent with their personal and professional beliefs.

Opportunities for Learning and Development

Job matches that provide opportunities for learning and professional development boost the satisfaction and engagement of job seekers. Job seekers seem to prefer positions that offer access to training programs, mentorship possibilities, and professional growth options (Lee and Kim, 2020). Organizations that prioritize learning and development enable job seekers to advance in their careers and realize their full potential, which in turn raises levels of commitment and satisfaction.

Compensation and Benefit Package

When assessing job matches, job seekers consider salary, bonuses, healthcare benefits, and work-life balance opportunities (Patel and Williams, 2022). Recruitment agencies that negotiate attractive compensation packages and advocate for their client's best interests contribute to the satisfaction of job seekers. These agencies guarantee fair and competitive compensation for job seeker's talents and efforts.

Long-Term Viability and Stability

Job seekers consider the long-term viability and stability of job matches when assessing their satisfaction with recruitment agencies. Johnson and Martinez (2019) highlight the importance of agencies presenting job seekers with roles in financially stable organizations with strong growth prospects and low turnover rates. Job seekers value agencies that prioritize matching them with roles that offer security, longevity, and opportunities for career advancement, minimizing the risk of job dissatisfaction and turnover in the future.

Timeliness and Responsiveness

This section explores the various facets of timeliness and responsiveness and how they impact the experiences of job seekers.

Components of Timeliness and Responsiveness

Application Response Time

Job seekers value prompt responses to their job applications, as it reflects the recruitment agency's level of engagement and commitment. Agencies that respond promptly demonstrate respect for job seekers' time and investment in the application process, fostering a positive impression and enhancing satisfaction levels.

Interview Scheduling and Coordination

A seamless and efficient hiring process depends on the effective scheduling and coordination of interviews. Job seekers value recruitment agencies that set up interviews quickly, avoid schedule issues, and give clear instructions about the procedures and expectations of the interview (Brown et al. 2021). Recruitment agencies need to be responsive in handling interviews in the hiring process since job seekers may become frustrated and disengaged if there are delays or misunderstandings in the scheduling of interviews.

Feedback and Communication

Keeping job seekers engaged and informed will require a considerable amount of feedback and communication from recruitment agencies. There is a positive relationship between job seeker's appreciation and regular feedback and communication from recruitment agencies. This implies that job seekers can manage expectations about an interview outcome when there is regular feedback and communication from recruitment agencies. It also helps job seekers gauge their progress in job search efforts.

Follow-Up after Interviews and Job Offers

According to Lee and Kim (2020), recruitment agencies must get in touch with job seekers as soon as possible following interviews to get their input, answer any queries or concerns, and provide them with an update on their candidacy. Recruitment agencies that aggressively and routinely follow up after interviews convey a sense of professionalism and attentiveness. Thereby allowing job seekers to have a positive perception of the agency and their overall experience.

Resolution of Issues and Concerns

Keeping trust and satisfaction requires prompt resolution of issues and concerns brought up by job seekers. Job seekers value organizations that respond to their questions or complaints in a timely and efficient manner since this shows a dedication to resolving problems and guaranteeing a great experience (Patel and Williams, 2022). Recruitment agencies that place a high priority on being responsive and proactively resolving issues or misconceptions with job seekers build deeper relationships with them. This raises satisfaction levels and increases the possibility of successful placements.

Adaptability and Flexibility

Throughout the recruitment process, job seekers place a high value on recruitment agencies that demonstrate adaptability and flexibility by adjusting their demands and preferences. According to Johnson and Martinez (2019), agencies must take into account job seeker's communication preferences, schedule restrictions, and any unanticipated events. Through the creation of a welcoming and accommodating environment that values job seeker's opinions and preferences, organizations that exhibit flexibility and a desire to meet individual requirements help to increase job seekers' happiness.

Conclusion

This chapter has provided a deep understanding of what job seekers require from recruitment agencies. The chapter holds that improving job seekers' satisfaction with recruitment agencies will require effective communication and transparency, quality job matches, timeliness, and responsiveness, amongst others.

Recruitment companies need to understand what makes job seekers satisfied to stay competitive and build lasting relationships. To meet job seeker's expectations, agencies should improve communication, match jobs better, respond quickly, and provide full support. Understanding the significance of these factors will assist job seekers in making wise choices while interacting with recruiting agencies.

Future research in the field of recruitment and job-seeking behavior may delve into several areas to expand this chapter's laid-out practices and information. Research can focus on the following areas:

Effectiveness of new technologies: Explore the impact of cutting-edge technologies, such as artificial intelligence and machine learning, on recruitment processes and job satisfaction.

Cross-cultural perspective: explore how cultural variations influence the expectations, preferences, and job seekers' satisfaction with recruitment agencies.

Long-term outcomes: Evaluate the long-term effects of recruitment agency services on employment success and job satisfaction. Examine the long-term outcomes and career paths of job seekers selected by recruitment agencies.

Scholars and practitioners may further improve our understanding of recruitment and job-search strategies by focusing on these research areas, which will eventually help both job seekers and recruiting firms.

Chapter 8:

The Role of Recruitment Agencies in the United States

9.0. Introduction

In the modern labor market, recruitment agencies play a significant role as intermediaries between organizations and potential employees. Recruitment agencies are also known as staffing agencies or employment agencies. They are agencies (organizations) that specialize in connecting job seekers with job opportunities offered by their clients (organizations). Recruitment agencies act as middlemen between job seekers looking to gain full or part-time employment and organizations looking to fill up vacancies. There are a range of services provided by recruitment agencies, and they include employee sourcing, interviewing, and placements.

The scope of recruitment agencies is broad, as it covers different industries, job roles and functions, employment arrangements (temporary, contractual, full-time, and casual), and executive search services. These agencies excel in talent acquisition, understanding industries, and networking with job seekers. This makes them highly effective and efficient in hiring for companies across various industries.

Recruitment agencies are valuable and relevant partners for organizations and job seekers. They provide numerous benefits that support and contribute to the labor market's efficiency. For instance, recruitment agencies help organizations save time and money by providing access to a larger pool of competent job seekers. By employing their specialized knowledge in applicant sourcing, screening, and matching, these agencies ensure that organizations engage top talents that fit the needs and demands of their corporate culture and values. Another benefit they bring to organizations is that they assist in navigating complex legal and regulatory regulations, which minimizes compliance risks associated with the recruitment and hiring process.

Furthermore, the benefits for job seekers include providing access to a broad selection of job openings, some of which may not be advertised on public job boards. Recruitment agencies offer personalized support and guidance to job seekers by helping them find opportunities that align with their desires. Also, prepare job seekers for interviews and negotiate employment offers. Also, they leverage their industry connections and insights to help job seekers find relevant opportunities that complement their career goals, qualifications, experiences, and competencies.

There are specific expectations that industries across the different sectors have of recruitment agencies. These expectations range from timeliness and efficiency to the quality of job seekers, industry knowledge and expertise, and communication and transparency. Let's discuss them briefly here. The first expectation is that recruitment agencies find qualified candidates within a set timeframe to meet staffing needs. Second, companies want skilled candidates with the right experience and qualifications to succeed in the role. To ensure this, agencies must conduct thorough screening and assessments.

Thirdly, the demand on recruitment agencies is the expectation that they have sound and grounded industry knowledge and expertise in the different sectors. For instance, knowledge of market trends, talent dynamics, and regulatory environments. Agencies are expected of agencies to use their knowledge and experience of the different industries to provide strategic direction and tailor-made recruitment and selection solutions that cater to the specific needs and challenges of their clients, which are organizations. Fourth, when partnering with recruitment agencies, organizations expect that communication will be transparent and well-defined. The expectation is that the lines of communication will be frequent and open to the progress made in the recruitment and selection process, and questions and concerns will be responded to promptly. Building confidence and fostering effective partnerships between organizations and recruitment agencies also requires transparency regarding contractual terms, fees, and candidates' information. Adherence to these industry expectations is important to recruitment agencies, as it necessitates building long-lasting and dependable partnerships with organizations. This chapter presents an exploration of the expectations of recruitment agencies by US organizations, the evolution of recruitment agencies, best practices, and prospects for the future.

9.1. The Evolution of Recruitment Agencies

In this session, the evolution of recruitment agencies is briefly explored by discussing the historical context, growth and development, and the current landscape.

Historical Context

In the United States, recruitment agencies have a rich history that dates back to the late nineteenth century. Recruitment agencies emerged during the Industrial Revolution when there was a high demand for a workforce. As industries began to expand, there was a missing link through which employers needed to connect with qualified workers. The missing link required an effective means, which necessitated the rise of the first recruitment agency. At the time, it was not called a recruitment agency; instead, it was referred to as a labor exchange or employment bureau.

A notable milestone in the beginning of a formalized approach toward recruitment and selection was the establishment of the US Employment Service in 1918, which was aimed at connecting World War I veterans with employment prospects. This was an important time for recruitment agencies to grow. Over the years, they have adapted to changes in the job market and new technology. After World War II, the demand for skilled workers increased sharply, leading agencies to expand and offer services in various industries. In the latter part of the twentieth century, recruitment agencies underwent significant transformations with the advent of computers and the Internet. Online job boards and portals, as well as other digital platforms, revolutionized the way job seekers and employers interacted, and they provided greater accessibility and efficiency in the recruitment and selection process.

Growth and Development

Several factors have contributed to the growth of US recruitment agencies. These factors include economic trends, demographic shifts, and the regulations of labor laws. As the economy diversified, recruitment agencies also diversified their services as a means to meet the changing demands of employers and job seekers. Furthermore, during the period of economic expansion, recruitment agencies played a significant role in facilitating workforce expansion in industries such as manufacturing, healthcare, finance, and technology.

Recruitment agencies provided services such as sourcing qualified candidates, conducting screenings and assessments, and assisting with the hiring process. Another contributing factor was the establishment of specialized recruitment agencies that focused on specific industries and job categories. These agencies gained extensive knowledge and expertise by attending networking events and specific marketplaces. They built networks involving agencies and industries within a niche market. Through their specialization, these recruitment agencies provide tailored solutions and meet the demands of employers by recruiting the right talents.

Additionally, globalization also helped to expand the operations of recruitment agencies across national borders. Examples of global recruitment agencies are Adecco, Randstad, Salesforce, AppleOne, Kforce, and Manpower. These agencies operate overseas to meet the demand for talent in emerging markets and facilitate cross-border recruitment.

Current Landscape

In today's world, the recruitment agency landscape in the US is characterized by competition and diversity. There are a wide range of agencies that cater to different industries, employment levels, and hiring requirements. Traditional brick-and-mortar agencies coexist with online job platforms and virtual interviewing techniques. AI hiring tools, data analytics, and virtual interviews are changing the recruitment industry. These technologies have made it easier to find and select candidates, improving efficiency and effectiveness of recruitment agencies' entire operations. Despite the benefits of technological innovation, human judgment and interaction are still essential in hiring decisions. Recruitment agencies actively work to build strong and healthy relationships with industries and job seekers. This is done by learning their needs and preferences and providing personalized support through the recruitment process.

9.2. Understanding Industry Expectations

In order to get a better understanding of industry expectations, we explore the challenges of talent acquisition, the role of recruitment agencies in addressing challenges, and the key metrics for success.

Challenges in Talent Acquisition

The talent acquisition challenges of 2023 are highlighted in a report by ZipRecruiter, which polled 2,000 hiring managers and talent acquisition professionals in the United States. The Chief Economist at ZipRecruiter, Julia Pollak, states that "employers continue to confront shortages of candidates with the right skills at the right price." "It makes sense for employers to invest in long-term solutions rather than band-aid fixes, as labor shortages are here to stay given current demographic trends."

Here are some of the challenges that recruiters face in acquiring talent.

Shortage of Talents

In the fast-rising technological world today, finding the right talent has become a major challenge for most recruiters. The reality is that there is not enough talent available in the market. There are fewer qualified candidates when compared to the rapidly changing demands for higher-level skills. In the top three recruitment challenges report by ZipRecruiter, 57 percent of organizations opined that there was a lack of qualified candidates, 46 percent said the talents were too few, and 41 percent said that they were unable to fill up a vacancy in the last six months because candidates wanted more salaries than they could offer. In 2024, the number one hiring challenge will be a shortage of talent, and the challenge is expected to get worse in the coming years. The McKinsey Global Institute report indicates that Europe and North America will need an estimated sixteen to eighteen million educated workers in the near future.

Diversity and Inclusion

Diversity, equality, and inclusion (DEI) continue to remain a major challenge in the recruitment and selection process for diverse reasons, which include unconscious bias or outright discrimination, systemic inequalities, and restricted access to opportunities. Despite efforts to address these challenges, they persist. According to ZipRecruiter, more than half of the organizations under review mentioned that DEI is a challenge because there is an absence of diversity in employee referrals. For instance, 50 percent of employers expressed that there was a lack of underrepresented candidates in the talent pipeline, 43 percent mentioned the lack of people of color, and 42 percent mentioned the lack of qualified women.

Competition for Talents

With the rise of the gig economy and the increasing mobility of the workforce, hiring the most talented candidates has become a major challenge for organizations. According to the ZipRecruiter report, 40 percent of employers mention that the competition for talent is from well-established and multinational corporations, and another 40 percent mention competition in terms of salaries and benefits. The reality is that the competition is stiff as organizations across different industries are competing for talent in the same talent pool.

Candidate Experience

A key factor in luring and keeping talent is the candidate's experience. Organizations need to ensure that the recruitment and selection process is positive and easy to navigate, from the initial stages of the application to onboarding and beyond. Qualified talents can be turned away by ineffective and irregular communication, protracted recruitment processes, and a lack of transparency, which can also cause harm to the reputation of the organization.

The Role of Recruitment Agencies in Addressing Talent Acquisition Challenges

Recruitment agencies play an important role in helping businesses overcome challenges related to acquiring talent and fulfilling their recruitment objectives. The knowledge, connections, and resources allow recruitment agencies to offer valuable and beneficial assistance in the following ways:

Talent Sourcing and Screening

Recruitment agencies use their extensive networks and databases to find and attract qualified talent for their clients. There are a good number of sourcing strategies, such as social media, job boards, recommendations, and networking, to reach out to both passive and active job seekers. Before candidates are offered to organizations, recruitment agencies carry out a comprehensive and rigorous screening and assessment process to evaluate the suitability of the candidates' experience, competence, and skills.

Market Insight and Trends

Recruitment agencies are well-versed in the dynamics of the labor market, the supply and demand for talents, and industry trends. They provide their clients with valuable information that helps them comprehend the state of the market, the tactics of their competitors, and new trends that could affect their talent acquisition plans. Agencies can foresee future talent demands and provide proactive solutions by staying abreast of industry trends.

Effective Diversity Recruitment Strategies

Effective diversity recruitment strategies are essential for building a diverse and inclusive workforce. Diversity, equality, and inclusion (DEI) promotion requires the effective and honest participation of recruitment agencies. Recruitment agencies can create and carry out DEI programs and work collaboratively with organizations to ensure targeted recruitment campaigns and inclusive job descriptions and adopt various approaches to find suitable and qualified candidates. Recruitment agencies can assist organizations in building a more diverse and representative team by actively seeking out candidates from underrepresented groups to foster inclusive recruitment and selection processes.

Enhancing Candidates' Experience

Throughout the recruitment process, recruitment agencies prioritize the experience of candidates. These agencies advocate for candidates by offering guidance, encouragement, support, and prompt feedback throughout the recruitment and selection process. Recruitment agencies also guarantee a courteous and positive experience by expediting the application process and facilitating communication between candidates and employers. Furthermore, these agencies are able to attract top talents and enhance their clients (organizations) brand reputation and image.

Key Metrics for Success

Recruitment agencies monitor key metrics in order to effectively assess the success of their recruitment and selection processes and show their clients (organizations) that they are valuable and reliable. These key metrics provide insight into the performance of their strategies, talent quality, and overall impact on different industrial sectors. The key metrics for success include the following:

Time to fill: This metric measures the average amount of time that passes between the start of a job request and the final candidate selection. In order to guarantee prompt satisfaction of their clients' staffing requirements and minimize losses associated with vacant positions, recruitment agencies strive to reduce the time to fill metric.

Quality of hire: This refers to how well recruitment agencies assess candidate performance and retention of candidates. To evaluate the effectiveness of their candidate sourcing and selection procedures, recruitment agencies monitor key performance indicators, tenure, and turnover rates. Effective hiring practices contribute to clients' (organizations) successes and provide long-term value and reliability.

Candidate satisfaction: This metric measures the satisfaction of job seekers' perceptions of recruitment agencies. Measures of job seeker satisfaction and areas for development include feedback surveys, job seekers' testimonials, and Net Promoter Scores (NPS). Positive experiences of job seekers boost referrals and recurring business purchases, as well as enhance the agency's reputation.

Client satisfaction: It measures the level of satisfaction with services provided by recruitment agencies to their clients. Recruitment agencies ask their clients for input on a range of topics related to the hiring process, such as communication, quality of talent, responsiveness, and overall service satisfaction ratings to encourage client retention and referrals, as well as foster strong partnerships.

Cost per hire: This measure counts the entire amount of money that clients spend when they successfully hire someone with the assistance of a recruiting agency. Cost per hire includes direct expenditures, such as advertising, agency fees, and candidate relocation expenses. Recruitment agencies optimize recruitment procedures and minimize expenses to provide their clients with optimal value and return on investment.

Recruitment agencies can assess their performance and effectiveness, identify areas for development, and demonstrate how these metrics affect their clients' talent acquisition strategies by tracking and evaluating these key performance indicators. To maintain a c, the recruitment and selection processes must be regularly evaluated, and processes must be regularly evaluated and improved.

9.3. Partnership Dynamics: Industry and Recruitment Agencies

The partnership dynamics between industry and recruitment agencies can be explained through three different approaches, which include collaboration, communication, transparency, and mutual accountability.

A. Collaborative Approach

Successful collaborations between industries and recruitment agencies are built on an effective collaborative approach that promotes mutual understanding, shared goals, and collective problem-sharing and solving. To ensure a successful alliance, industries, and recruitment agencies will require alignment in their goals, open communication, knowledge sharing, flexibility, and adaptability.

When aligning objectives, both industries and recruitment agencies ensure they understand the type and quality of job seekers they want to recruit. Also, the alignment of objectives creates the opportunity for reducing the hiring period, increasing workforce diversity, and saving costs. Industries and recruitment agencies tend to benefit from each other's resources and strengths when it comes to achieving the best outcomes in the recruitment and selection process.

In addition to the alignment of goals, there is a need for the different industries and recruitment agencies to keep the channels of communication open in a transparent and genuine manner. For instance, there should be regular meetings, status reporting and updates, and feedback sessions held to smooth continuous communication and ensure that priorities and expectations are in order. Open communication builds trust and strengthens relationships over time. Another key benefit of collaboration is knowledge sharing. Industries and recruitment agencies can exchange valuable insights, market trends, and best practices. By working together, recruitment agencies provide industries with data on talent availability, competitive analysis, and market trends, helping to refine recruitment strategies. In response, the industries share information about their corporate culture, employment standards and practices, and projected workforce requirements. Collaboratively, industries and recruitment agencies make better judgments and informed decisions that inform their approach toward the ever-changing dynamics of the labor market.

Bear in mind that a collaborative partnership is characterized by its ability to be flexible and adaptable to accommodate the changing needs and challenges in the labor market. In this way, industries and recruitment agencies should be willing to regulate strategies, processes, and deadlines in response to shifting job seeker preferences, market dynamics, and corporate priorities. Both industries and recruitment agencies can overcome obstacles and take advantage of new opportunities when presented with flexibility and adaptability.

B. Communication and Transparency

Effective communication and transparency are important approaches for achieving success in a partnership. Having open and honest communication promotes trust, improves teamwork, and limits misconceptions and miscommunication. In a partnership defined by effective communication and transparency, there are

191

bound to be clear expectations, timely updates, feedback mechanisms, and transparency in fees and agreements.

At the start of a collaborative partnership, both parties expressly state their roles, responsibilities, and expectations. For instance, both the industry and recruitment agency will be clear about the qualifications, skills, and competence they require from job seekers, the timeline for recruitment, communication protocols, and performance evaluation. Setting clear expectations ensures alignment in partnerships and minimizes uncertainties in the recruitment process. Along with clarity, regular and timely communication is essential throughout hiring. Recruitment agencies should keep industries informed with updates on candidate sourcing, screening, interview scheduling, and feedback. Similarly, industries provide recruitment agencies with feedback on candidates' suitability, hiring decisions, and modifications to hiring priorities. Engaging in practices based on timely updates will allow industries and recruitment agencies to make informed decisions and stay informed.

More so, partnerships require feedback, as it is essential to the continuous improvement and optimization of the recruitment and selection process. For example, industries and recruitment agencies exchange feedback on key aspects such as top talent, communication effectiveness, and overall satisfaction. Over time, constructive feedback helps identify areas for improvement and improves the partnership. Additionally, transparent communication about fees, contracts, and service agreements fosters stronger and more positive collaborations. Most recruitment agencies provide a clear outline of the fee structure, payment terms, and any additional services or upfront charges. In turn, industries provide clarity on their budget constraints, invoicing procedures, and expectations regarding service delivery. Transparent and open pricing agreements reduce disagreements and promote cooperative working relationships built on trust.

C. Mutual Accountability

Mutual accountability in partnerships requires both parties to set clear objectives, role clarity, performance metrics, and continuous improvement. The collaborative partnership between industries and recruitment agencies requires establishing clear, measurable, and achievable objectives. These objectives include hiring targets, performance indicators, and an activity schedule for recruitment processes. Having well-defined goals makes it possible for both parties to monitor progress and measure outcomes in an efficient and effective manner.

Similarly, industries and recruitment agencies need to have a good understanding of their roles, responsibilities, and accountability. Recruitment agencies are accountable for sourcing, screening, and presenting qualified candidates to the industries; on the other hand, industries are responsible for providing feedback, making hiring decisions, and onboarding chosen candidates. Role clarity has the benefit of reducing ambiguity and guaranteeing accountability for outcomes.

Another way to reinforce mutual accountability in partnerships is to apply performance metrics and indicators (KPIs) to track progress and evaluate outcomes. For instance, recruitment agencies measure their performance against metrics such as time-to-fill, quality of candidates, client satisfaction, and retention rates. While industries evaluate the effectiveness of recruitment agencies on their ability to meet hiring targets, quality candidates, and the value added to the recruitment and selection process through performance metrics, industries, and recruitment agencies are able to hold each other accountable for achieving desired outcomes.

Mutual accountability fosters an environment that encourages continuous learning and improvement in the partnership. What this means is that industries and recruitment agencies proactively seek feedback, analyze performance data, and identify opportunities for optimization and improvements. For instance, initiatives for continuous improvement can include knowledge-sharing sessions, technology upgrades, training and development programs, and hiring process refinements. Adopting a mindset of continuous improvement helps partnerships propel innovation and creativity, boost productivity, and improve the overall quality of the collaboration.

9.4. Industry-Specific Expectations

In exploring the industry-specific expectations, the chapter examines the technological sector, the healthcare industry, and finance and banking.

A. Technological Sector

The technology sector is one of the most dynamic and rapidly evolving industries because it is driven by constant innovation, digital transformation, and the constant demand for new skills. It is a highly competitive sector, and as such, there is a high demand for recruitment agencies to be significant in identifying, attracting, and retaining top talents for organizations operating in the sector. Some of the technology sector-specific expectations include demand for specialized skills, cultural fit assessment, agile recruitment processes, and diversity, equality, and inclusion (DEI) initiatives.

Demand for Specialized Skills

There are different subfields within the technological sector. Some of these subfields include software development, cybersecurity, data analysis, artificial intelligence, and cloud computing. Organizations operating within the sector are constantly searching for new talents who have specialized technical skills and are at expert levels in emerging technologies. There is a need for recruitment agencies to constantly update their knowledge about the technology sector by learning about the latest trends, technologies, and tools if they are to remain relevant. It is only with updated knowledge and awareness that recruitment agencies can effectively source candidates with the right qualifications, skills, and competence to meet the demands of IT organizations.

Assessing Cultural Fit

Cultural fit plays a crucial role in the recruitment process for technology organizations because the potential candidate should be able to adapt to and function effectively with the culture and values of the organization's working environment. While specialized skills are important, technological organizations consider that potential candidates should be willing and ready to work collaboratively with teams, be self-sufficient, and be creative in their approach to work. Therefore, recruitment agencies should go beyond technical skills and assess candidates' soft skills, communication style, problem-solving abilities, and adaptability to the company's culture and team dynamics.

Agile Recruitment Processes

There is a need for recruitment agencies to be flexible, responsive, and agile to meet the demands of the fast-paced global environment of the technology sector. Organizations within the technology sector are constantly competing for top talents to work in the evolving landscape. Bear in mind that the technology sector has high business frequency because of its competitive market nature. Therefore, recruitment agencies need to streamline their processes or optimize their workforce, engage technology for efficiency, and maintain open communication channels with organizations and candidates to guarantee quick and positive recruitment outcomes.

Diversity, Equality, and Inclusion (DEI) Initiatives

DEI is a topical issue in the US, and the technology sector has had historical and constant challenges with DEI, which cover gender imbalance, underrepresentation of minority groups, and a lack of inclusivity in its workplace culture. Recruitment agencies have a significant role to play in supporting organizations with DEI initiatives by sourcing and promoting diverse candidates, advocating for inclusive hiring practices, and helping organizations create a welcoming and equitable work environment.

B. Healthcare Sector

The healthcare sector is situated in a complex regulatory environment, which demands skilled healthcare professionals and engagement in critical missions. The healthcare sector poses unique challenges and expectations for recruitment agencies as they attempt to meet the staffing needs of hospitals, clinics, medical practices, and other healthcare organizations. The healthcare sector's specific expectations include regulatory compliance, DEI initiatives, candidate experience, and technological adoption.

Regulatory Compliance

Strict federal and state regulatory standards heavily regulate the healthcare sector. Strict federal and state regulatory standards, including credentialing and licensure, govern the sector. To preserve compliance and reduce risks for organizations, there is a need for recruitment agencies to subject candidates to background checks, drug screening, verification of credentials, and all other necessary legal criteria.

Diversity, Equality, and Inclusion (DEI) Initiatives

The healthcare industry is seeking to build diverse and inclusive teams that reflect the larger part of society in the US. It is believed that implementing DEI can help provide culturally competent care that is sensitive to cultural differences, free of suspicion, and widely accepted by the different communities in the US. The role of recruitment agencies is crucial in supporting DEI initiatives, and they can achieve this by sourcing diverse candidates from all ethnicities and communities in the US, addressing unconscious bias in the hiring process, and promoting an inclusive workplace culture.

Candidate Experience

There is a high demand for specialized skills in the healthcare sector, and it is competitive. The demand for skilled professionals is less than the supply, as there are shortages of qualified healthcare professionals. In light of this, recruitment agencies source qualified and experienced professionals from within and globally to fill the high demand. To ensure top professionals are recruited, agencies should guarantee the provision of personalized support for candidates in a timely manner. Ensuring a smooth transition into the new position will help attract and retain top healthcare professionals.

Technological Adoption

Digital transformation has taken over all sectors of the economy, including healthcare. The healthcare sector has adopted telemedicine, electronic health records (EHRs), and other technology-enabling solutions to improve operational efficiency and effectiveness while improving patient care services and delivery. In order to catch up with the times, recruitment agencies should attend industry network events, stay updated with the latest trends in technological advancement, and help organizations in the sector navigate the complexities of hiring candidates with technological know-how and expertise.

C. Finance and Banking Sectors

Finance and banking are high-stakes industries that are regularly scrutinized and constantly seeking top talents with specialized skills in finance, accounting, risk management, and compliance. In the banking and finance sectors, recruitment agencies are important partners in assisting financial organizations in identifying, attracting, and retaining qualified candidates who understand the intricacies of the industry. The industry's expectations include risk management, confidentiality and data security, speed and accuracy in recruitment, and regulatory compliance.

Risk Management

Risk management is a top priority in banking and finance because of the consequences that may arise from noncompliance with regulations, financial losses, and reputational damage. As part of the skills and expertise that recruitment agencies will demand from potential candidates, risk management will be essential. Other skills that will be in high demand include financial analysis, fraud prevention, and regulatory knowledge. Financial institutions require these skills to mitigate risks and safeguard their assets.

Data Security and Confidentiality

Financial institutions handle proprietary and sensitive customer data, which necessitates strict confidentiality and data security measures. Recruitment agencies must adhere to stringent privacy and security protocols to protect organizations and candidate information throughout the recruitment process. This entails putting in place access restrictions, encryption protocols, and secure data storage systems to protect private information from disclosure or unwanted access.

Speedy and Accurate

To meet the staffing demands of organizations and stay competitive, recruitment agencies must operate with accuracy and speed in the fast-paced world of banking and finance. Financial institutions are always in need of urgent hiring to fill positions in investment banking, asset management, and financial advisory services. Furthermore, to facilitate rapid placements without compromising quality or compliance, recruitment agencies should optimize their workflow, make effective use of technology, and keep a pool of prescreened candidates.

Regulatory Compliance

The finance and banking industries are subject to complex regulatory frameworks, some of which include federal and state laws, industry standards, and compliance requirements. Recruitment agencies must thoroughly verify candidates. Agencies should ensure that candidates hold the requisite qualifications, certifications, and licenses in order to adhere to industry best practices and regulations. Recruitment agencies will carry out exhaustive background checks on candidates, verify their credentials, and stay informed of any modifications to the law that may impact the hiring process.

9.5. Adapting to Changing Industry Trends

There are two areas that are trending at the moment: remote work and technological advancement.

A. Remote Work Dynamics

In recent years, there has been a paradigm shift in the concept of remote work. Global events like the COVID-19 pandemic have accelerated this process. In order to effectively serve hiring organizations and job seekers, recruitment agencies must adjust to the evolving realities of the modern workplace as more organizations adopt remote work arrangements. Because of remote employment, recruitment agencies face challenges and opportunities in sourcing, screening, and placing individuals in virtual work settings. The chapter discusses the following in the diagram below:

Source: Designed for the book

Remote Work Trends and Adoption

Due to technological breakthroughs, shifting employee preferences, and the necessity of maintaining business continuity in the face of unforeseen circumstances, remote work has become more common across different industries. There are research findings that indicate that a sizeable section of the workforce now favors remote or hybrid work arrangements, with employers providing more flexibility in an effort to attract and retain top talents. Recruitment agencies must be abreast of the latest developments in remote work and adopt rates to align their services with the changing needs of organizations and job seekers.

Virtual Recruitment Processes

There is a need to adopt virtual recruitment processes because of the transformation of traditional recruitment processes brought about by the shift towards remote work. There are various channels that are in place to enable recruitment agencies to engage with job seekers and facilitate the hiring process. Examples of these channels include online assessments, virtual interviews, and video conferences. Despite the geographical distance, recruitment agencies conduct virtual interviews, analyze the abilities and skill levels of candidates, and assess cultural fit using digital platforms and remote communication technologies. Adopting these remote channels ensures that recruiting processes remain consistent.

Candidate Assessment and Onboarding

Remote work dynamics require recruitment agencies to adapt their candidate assessment and onboarding processes to virtual environments. Agencies employ innovative approaches such as online simulation, virtual assessments, and remote orientation programs to evaluate the suitability of job seekers for remote work and transition into virtual work environments. Efficient evaluation and orientation procedures are pivotal in guaranteeing that job seekers have the required competencies and assistance to prosper in remote work environments.

Flexibility and Adaptability

In approaching talent acquisition, recruitment agencies must be flexible and adaptable, given the realities of remote work. In order to meet the needs and preferences of remote workers, agencies must modify their sourcing methods, candidate engagement strategies, and recruitment workflows. Meeting the demands of organizations and candidates in remote work environments requires flexibility in the scheduling of interviews, the administration of tests, and the organization of onboarding activities. Recruiting agencies may provide value-added services suited to remote work dynamics and gain stakeholders' trust by demonstrating agility and responsiveness.

Technology and Infrastructure

Technology is critical for supporting virtual recruitment and the ability to operate remotely. ATS, video conferencing software, candidate tracking systems, and collaboration platforms are just a few examples of the digital tools and platforms that recruitment agencies use to help with remote communication, document sharing, and candidate management. To guarantee the security, dependability, and scalability of remote work activities, substantial investments in cybersecurity and technological infrastructure are necessary. Recruiting agencies may improve remote work processes, foster teamwork, and provide hiring organizations and candidates with smooth experiences by utilizing technology wisely.

Establishing Remote Work Policies and Ensuring Compliance

Recruiting agencies must deal with legal and regulatory compliance obligations related to remote work arrangements. It is imperative for recruitment agencies to guarantee adherence to labor laws, data protection regulations, and employment standards that are relevant to remote work settings. To mitigate risks and maintain transparency with clients and candidates, it is crucial to communicate clearly about remote work regulations, contractual agreements, and compliance measures. Recruitment agencies can reduce any legal risks related to remote work arrangements and increase their reputation and confidence with stakeholders.

Overall, the dynamics of remote work have become integral to the contemporary workplace, influencing the way recruitment agencies function and provide services in an online environment. By adopting virtual recruitment processes, embracing remote work trends, and placing a high value on flexibility and adaptability, recruitment agencies can successfully navigate the opportunities and challenges of remote work environments and provide value-added solutions that satisfy changing client and candidate needs in a digitally native world.

B. Impact of Technological Advancement

Technological advancements have completely changed the recruitment sector by transforming traditional practices, processes, and approaches. These technological advancements, which range from data analytics to artificial intelligence (AI), have significantly changed how recruiting agencies function and provide services to hiring organizations and candidates. The diagram below depicts the main areas in which advances in technology have had a notable impact:

Source: Designed for the study

Recruitment Processes Can Be Automated

Automation has improved efficiency and reduced costs for recruitment agencies by streamlining a number of the recruiting process's components. Recruiters may concentrate on more strategic endeavors by delegating monotonous duties like résumé screening, interview scheduling, and candidate sourcing to AI-powered tools and algorithms. Because of automated workflows, recruitment agencies can more efficiently satisfy the staffing needs of hiring organizations, ensuring consistency, minimizing manual errors, and shortening the time to fill.

AI-Powered Candidate Matching

AI-driven candidate-matching algorithms examine a vast amount of data to find the best candidates for particular job tasks. Recruiters can make better hiring judgments by using these algorithms to compare candidates' skills, qualifications, experience, and cultural fit to job criteria. AI-powered matching algorithms raise the possibility of successful hiring decisions, lessen bias in the selection process, and improve the quality of candidate matches.

Predictive Analytics for Talent Acquisition

Predictive analytics is a useful tool in talent acquisition because it can estimate future talent needs and recruitment outcomes based on previous data, trends, and patterns. Recruitment agencies use predictive analytics to anticipate shifts in the labor market's dynamics, spot new skill gaps, and proactively address personnel shortages. These agencies can create proactive recruitment strategies, modify sourcing approaches, and coordinate their efforts with organizations' long-term hiring requirements.

Video Interviews and Assessment Platforms

These tools enable recruiting agencies to interview and evaluate job seekers virtually, removing geographical constraints and streamlining the virtual hiring process. These systems give recruiters important insights into job seekers' communication skills, problem-solving ability, and cultural fit. Examples of these systems are recorded interviews, live video interviews, and interactive evaluations. Video interviewing systems streamline the hiring process, shorten the time to hire, and improve job seekers' experiences by providing more flexibility and convenience.

Data-Driven Decision-Making

Data analytics tools may assist recruitment agencies in gathering, evaluating, and interpreting data, allowing them to make better decisions and streamline their recruitment strategies. Data analytics is a tool that recruitment companies use to monitor key performance indicators, assess the efficiency of sourcing channels, and identify areas where the hiring process needs improvement. In order to improve results for customers and applicants, agencies can use data-driven insights to inform choices, allocate resources more effectively, and enhance recruitment procedures over time.

Enhanced Candidate Experience

The candidate experience has become more engaging, individualized, and interactive because of technological advancements. Recruiting firms use technology to give candidates a smooth and simple experience from first contact to onboarding in the recruitment process. In a competitive market, interactive chatbots, mobile-friendly apps, and tailored communication platforms distinguish agencies as employers of choice, improve candidate engagement, and reduce application process friction.

In all, the recruitment sector has experienced a significant transformation due to technological advancements, which have improved efficiency, revolutionized processes, and produced better results for hiring organizations, candidates, and recruiting agencies. Recruiting agencies, with the help of technologies, can remain ahead of the curve, adjust to shifting market trends, and provide value-added services that satisfy their stakeholders' changing expectations in a digital ecosystem that is changing quickly.

9.6. Best Practices for Recruitment Agencies

A. Tailored Recruitment Strategies

To meet the needs and demands of organizations and job seekers, recruitment agencies need to implement tailored recruitment strategies to ensure success. Here, the recommended practices for developing recruitment strategies include needs assessment, targeted candidate sourcing, and personalized candidate engagement.

Needs Assessment

The first stage in developing a tailored recruitment strategy is to conduct a comprehensive evaluation of each client's hiring needs, corporate culture, and recruitment preferences. It is important for recruitment companies to work closely with customers to comprehend their staffing needs, ideal applicant profiles, and business goals. By implementing a needs assessment, recruitment agencies can tailor their strategies and provide solutions that complement the priorities and goals of their clients.

Targeted Candidate Sourcing

Targeted candidate sourcing is one of the strategies recruitment agencies use to entice candidates with the appropriate qualifications, competencies, skills, and fit for particular positions. Some of the sourcing channels are job boards, social media, professional networking events, and industry events. Recruitment agencies can optimize their endeavors and augment the probability of promptly locating competent candidates by focusing on different candidate sourcing avenues.

Personalized Candidate Engagement

To develop rapport, foster trust, and keep candidates in constant contact during the recruiting process, effective recruitment tactics incorporate personalized candidate engagement techniques. Recruiting agencies should adjust their communication style (phone, email, or in-person meetings) to the preferences and priorities of each candidate. Personalized interaction improves the overall candidate experience and demonstrates a commitment to the candidates' needs.

B. Candidate Relationship Management (CRM)

Candidate Relationship Management (CRM) is a fundamental component of effective recruitment agencies, which enables them to establish and maintain relationships with candidates over time. Some of the top practices recruitment agencies use to effectively manage job seeker's relationships include a candidate-centered approach, proactively talent pipelining, and relationship building. The explanations for these practices are as follows:

Candidate-Centred Approach

This requires prioritizing the needs, preferences, and career aspirations of job seekers throughout the process of recruitment and selection. Recruitment agencies make an effort to offer job seekers personalized support, prompt feedback, and open contact to guarantee that the experience is positive and satisfactory.

Developing a Proactive Talent Pipeline

It is the process through which recruitment agencies identify, engage, interact with, and nurture potential job seekers for future job opportunities. It is crucial for recruitment agencies to maintain their top talent pipeline by consistently sourcing, screening, and engaging with passive job seekers who have desirable qualifications, competencies, and skills. By creating and managing a talent pipeline, recruitment agencies can reduce the time it takes to fill job vacancies, enhance the quality of talent, and strengthen relationships with organizations.

Relationship Building

In order to establish rapport, trust, and credibility with job seekers, effective CRM will require continuous relationship building. Recruitment agencies should invest time and be committed to building organic and authentic relationships with job seekers in order to understand their professional goals, motivations, and desires in the working environment and culture of the intended organizations. It is possible that recruitment agencies can improve engagements, boost referrals, and provide long-term value for both job seekers and organizations by building healthy relationships.

C. Continuous Learning and Development

Recruitment agencies must encourage investment in continuous learning and development, as it is important for keeping abreast of industry trends, technological advancements, and best practices in talent acquisition. Therefore, to encourage continuous learning and development, recruitment agencies should adopt these strategies: training and skill development, knowledge sharing and collaboration, industry networking, and professional development.

Training and Skill Development

Recruitment agencies should invest in training and skills development programs to improve the proficiencies of their recruitment teams. Training programs should include sourcing techniques, interviewing skills, candidate assessment methods, and industry-specific knowledge. Regular training and skill development ensure that recruitment agency employees stay updated with evolving hiring practices. Also, the agencies will be able to provide high-quality services to job seekers and organizations.

Effective Knowledge Sharing and Collaboration

Promoting knowledge and collaboration among team members helps to create an environment where learning never stops inside an agency. In order to allow team members to share ideas, best practices, and lessons discovered from their recruitment experiences, recruitment agencies need to organize frequent team gatherings, brainstorming sessions, and knowledge-sharing seminars. When recruitment agencies collaborate, they can make use of their collective knowledge, address challenges more effectively and efficiently, and promote innovation in talent acquisition.

Industry Networking and Professional Development

Recruitment agencies should encourage staff members to participate in industry networking events, conferences, and opportunities for professional development. Through networking, recruiters can build and expand professional networks, build healthy relationships and partnerships with job seekers and hiring organizations, and stay informed about current trends in the industry for talent acquisition. Conferences and workshops for professional development offer seamless learning opportunities for new ideas, technologies, and best practices in hiring and selection.

Furthermore, continuous learning and development presents an avenue through which recruitment agencies can provide their teams with the knowledge, skills, and resources needed to thrive in a competitive recruitment landscape. It also helps recruiting teams provide excellent value to both job seekers and their clients (hiring organizations).

9.7. Overcoming Challenges

There are challenges that recruitment agencies are confronted with. Here, we explore three main challenges and how recruitment agencies can overcome them.

A. Talent Shortage

Talent shortages are one of the foremost problems confronting recruitment agencies. Although there are millions of job seekers, their quality, competence, experience, and skills are below par to meet the demands of organizations. To remedy this situation, we recommend the following strategies:

Talent Pipelining

Recruitment agencies can reduce the effects of a talent shortage by proactively creating and managing a talent pipeline of top talent. Through consistent sourcing, engagement, networking, and nurturing of potential candidates; recruitment agencies could guarantee a consistent pool of talent to fulfill organizational needs and demands.

Skill Development Programs

Investments in training initiatives and skill development programs can help address and close the skills gaps and shortages in the workforce pool. Recruitment agencies can also offer training for job seekers to get them up-to-date and acquainted with specialized skills and job functions in different industrial sectors. Some of the initiatives may include training workshops, upskilling programs, and certificate courses. These educational and skills programs can help job seekers become more competitive in the job market and more attractive to clients.

Utilizing a Variety of Sourcing Channels

Recruitment agencies can access untapped talent pools and overcome talent shortages when they diversify their sourcing channels.

Sourcing channels such as job boards, social media, professional networks, referrals, and networking events. The use of different sourcing channels can help agencies improve their chances of discovering talented candidates who may be actively looking for work.

B. Competition from In-House Recruitment Teams

Recruitment agencies face competition from in-house recruitment teams, as many organizations have their own internal recruitment teams to reduce costs and expedite the hiring process. To overcome the challenges of the competition, recruitment agencies can adopt the following strategies, which are explained below:

Specialization and Expertise

Recruitment agencies can set themselves apart from in-house recruitment teams by concentrating and specializing in niche industries, roles, or talent markets in which they are well-versed and possess extensive industry knowledge. Recruitment agencies may provide value to organizations and draw in those who are looking for specialized staffing solutions by providing specialized recruitment services.

Value-Added Services

In order to set themselves apart from in-house recruitment teams, recruitment agencies can offer value-added services that go beyond traditional staffing solutions. Some examples of value-added services include talent mapping, market research, employer branding, and workforce planning consulting. Recruitment agencies can establish themselves as valued partners and trusted advisors by providing comprehensive solutions that cater to the strategic talent needs of their clients.

Technology and Innovation

Leveraging technology and innovation may help recruitment agencies improve their effectiveness, efficiency, and competitive advantage. Recruitment agencies may enhance applicants' experiences, quicken recruitment processes, and provide better results for different organizations through investments in cutting-edge technologies like AI-powered sourcing tools, predictive analytics platforms, and video interviewing software. Furthermore, through investments in technology and innovation, recruitment agencies will provide creative solutions, which will set them apart from in-house recruitment teams.

C. Regulatory Compliance

Some difficulties confront recruitment agencies when it comes to regulatory compliance because of the several laws they have to confirm at the federal, state, and industry levels. All of these laws control the recruitment and selection processes, as well as the placement of candidates. However, there are tactics that recruiting agencies can use to overcome regulatory compliance. These tactics include staying informed, establishing policies and procedures, and partnering with legal experts.

Staying Informed

Recruitment agencies must stay informed of all changes in labor laws, employment regulations, industry regulations, standards, and practices that may affect their operations. There is a need to regularly monitor updates from industry associations, regulatory bodies, and legal experts to ensure compliance with pertinent laws and regulations.

Establishing Policies and Procedures

Robust policies and procedures enable recruitment agencies to maintain compliance with regulatory requirements. To maintain legal compliance and mitigate risks, agencies should ensure that policies and procedures for data security, employment verification, background checks, and candidate screening are clearly defined.

Partner with Legal Expertise

Seeking the services of legal and professional expertise is beneficial when recruitment agencies are presented with intricate regulatory matters. Legal experts can assist recruitment agencies with the interpretation and application of relevant rules and regulations, risk assessment, and the implementation of suitable countermeasures to reduce legal exposure.

In summary, recruitment agencies can efficiently overcome regulatory challenges and maintain high standards of ethical and legal conduct in their operations by investing in compliance management and putting practical methods into practice.

9.8. Future Outlook

A. Exploring the Emerging Trends in Recruitment's Future

The future of recruitment looks bright, as there will be trends that are revolutionary in the industry. Some of these trends will include artificial intelligence, automation technologies, remote work, and virtual recruitment.

AI and automation technologies: These trends will continue to be crucial in optimizing the recruitment process, that is, from candidate sourcing and screening to interview scheduling and onboarding. AI-powered solutions will boost productivity, enhance job seekers' experiences, and make data-driven talent acquisition decisions possible.

Remote work and virtual recruitment: The shift toward remote work and virtual recruitment came to the fore during the global pandemic of COVID-19. Remote work and virtual recruitment will become commonplace in the near future as individuals seek more freedom from office workspaces. Virtual recruitment practices such as virtual job fairs, online tests, and video interviews will become commonplace methods for interacting with applicants and streamlining the hiring process across national boundaries.

B. Opportunities for Innovation

In the future, the recruitment sector will have a plethora of opportunities for innovation and business disruption in the recruitment sector in the future. By leveraging predictive analytics and embracing diversity, equality, and inclusion, recruitment agencies can benefit.

Leveraging predictive analytics: Predictive analytics is a method of using data to project future results. This process uses statistical models, AI, data analysis, and machine learning to identify patterns that may predict future behavior. In recruitment, predictive analysis leverages data insights to anticipate talent trends, understand job seekers' preferences, and improve hiring strategies.

Embracing diversity, equality, and inclusion: This will involve giving diversity and inclusion programs a top priority, as it will help recruitment agencies attract top talents from underrepresented groups. It will create a diverse and equal opportunity for all job seekers and drive innovation and creativity in organizations.

C. Potential Disruptions and Challenges

Although there are innovative opportunities in the future of recruitment, there is also a need for recruitment agencies to prepare for possible disruptions and challenges. Some of these challenges could consist of talent scarcity and regulatory changes.

Talent scarcity: The future of work looks very dour as more people are choosing to define their work in the entrepreneur space. Already, industries are experiencing a high demand for quality talent in specialized fields, which is posing a challenge for recruitment agencies. The future does not seem any better, as it is projected that recruitment agencies will continue to experience challenges in sourcing and attracting top-quality talents to meet organizational demands.

Regulatory changes: Recruitment agencies may face challenges in maintaining legal compliance, data security, and moral hiring processes due to changing regulatory environments and compliance standards. In order to keep up with changes in regulations and modify their procedures accordingly in order to reduce risks and uphold compliance.

9.9. Conclusion

This chapter has provided a comprehensive exploration of the role of recruitment agencies in the US. The chapter provides deep discussions on the evolution of recruitment agencies, industry expectations, partnership dynamics, challenges, and future outlook. As best practices, discussions focused on candidate relationship management, specialized recruitment strategies, and continuous learning. The future developments for the sector to consider include diversity, remote work, and artificial intelligence (AI).

Furthermore, aligning with industry standards is important for recruitment agencies to thrive. In the evolving landscape of recruitment, it is necessary to gain adequate knowledge and understanding of industry needs, collaborative partnerships, and provision of value-added services for sustained growth and success. In conclusion, recruitment agencies should accept change, be creative, and adjust to changing market trends and organization demands. Recruitment agencies can handle challenges and take advantage of opportunities through maintaining flexibility and adaptability, effectively utilizing technology, and prioritizing continuous improvement.

Chapter 9:
Dos and Don'ts of Recruitment

10.0. Introduction

The foundation for any successful organization is effective recruitment, which is also essential to building a strong and productive workforce. Recruitment is more important than staffing because it has a bigger impact on an organization's trajectory and overall health. Effective hiring is crucial for two main reasons: first, it has a significant impact on organizational success, and second, it is essential for assembling a powerful team.

Effective recruitment practices have a direct impact on an organization's capacity to meet its goals and objectives. The caliber of people a company hires affects its ability to create new ideas, keep valuable knowledge, and stay competitive. A well-planned hiring process aligns employees with the company's goals, ensuring each new hire adds important skills needed for success. More so, effective hiring also reduces turnover and spars organizations from the costly and disruptive effects of constant staff changes. Organizations may improve their adaptability, agility, and long-term sustainability in a dynamic business environment.

Furthermore, the foundation of organizational productivity and innovation is a solid and cohesive team. Recruitment is essential to the process that brings together people with different skill sets, experiences, and perspectives to create a collaborative environment that encourages innovation and problem-solving. Hence, carefully choosing team members guarantees that each member balances out the shortcomings of the others and enhances their strengths, resulting in a balanced and harmonious synergy. A strong team not only does better work but also creates a positive workplace, keeping employees happy, involved, and more likely to stay. A good hiring process not only fills jobs but also builds a team that works better together than individually.

The goal of this chapter is to provide a thorough examination of recruitment dos and don'ts in order to provide organizations with practical insights and strategies to improve their recruitment practices. There are two primary sections in this chapter, each with a subheading that highlights different areas of focus. The dos section covers important topics, such as job analysis, sourcing strategies, application processes, screening and assessment, transparent communication, diversity, equality, and inclusion (DEI). On the other hand, the don't section explores common mistakes such as neglecting employer branding, rushing the hiring process, overlooking candidate experience, neglecting legal compliance, relying solely on technology, and failing to adapt to market trends. The chapter concludes with a summary of the main points and the need for continuous development in the recruitment process for long-term organizational performance.

10.1. The Dos of Recruitment

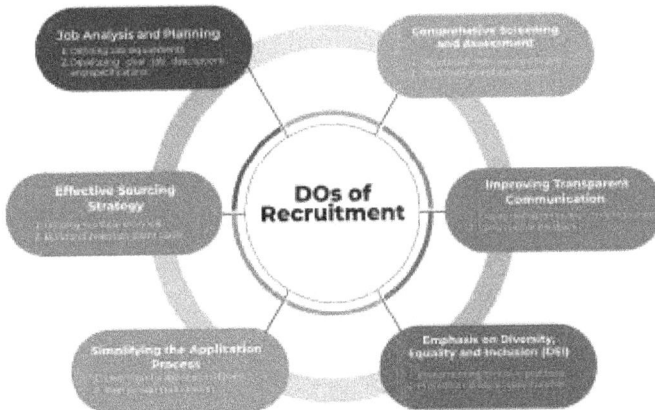

Source: Designed by Author

1. Job Analysis and Planning

A thorough process of job analysis and planning is the first step toward effective recruitment. It also forms the basis of effective talent acquisition initiatives. Job analysis and planning involve two critical components: defining the job requirement and developing clear job descriptions and specifications, as these will help organizations recruit the most talented applicants.

1.1. Defining Job Requirements

Defining job requirements allows organizations to attract job applicants with the right competencies, qualities, and skills, as this will help optimize job performance. Clearly defining job requirements means briefly but thoroughly explaining the role's duties, goals, and expected results. This helps companies avoid hiring people who aren't the right fit for the job. Here, companies focus on conducting thorough job analysis and identifying the key skills and qualifications.

1.1a. Conducting Job Analysis

A job analysis is a systematic process of collecting, documenting, and analyzing information that pertains to a job. It is important to conduct a thorough job analysis to identify the precise work needs. Different techniques are used to analyze jobs, and they include interviews, observations, questionnaires, and task analysis. An extensive job analysis guarantees that the needs of the position are in line with the goals and objectives of the company, thereby enabling the company to determine and identify the qualifications and skills necessary to achieve success in the position.

1.1b. Identifying the Skills and Qualifications

A critical aspect of defining job requirements is to identify the skills and qualifications of job applicants. Companies need to distinguish between essential and desirable qualifications and skills when screening and interviewing applicants. The skills and qualifications entail having both technical and interpersonal competencies that are relevant to the job. Organizations ensure that the right applicants are selected for the job by identifying their skills and qualifications. Also, taking into consideration factors such as educational qualifications, levels of experience, certifications, and job-related competencies guarantees that applicants fulfill the minimal requirements for the position.

1.2. Develop Clear Job descriptions and specifications

In developing clear job descriptions and specifications, two aspects come to mind. These are the use of specific and concise language and the emphasis on core responsibilities and expectations.

1.2a. The Use of Specific and Concise Language

It is important to use specific and concise wording when creating job descriptions and specifications. Clear language helps applicants gain a deeper understanding of the job role, expected outcomes, and the necessary qualifications and experiences to succeed on the job. Use terminologies that accurately reflect the job description and specifications to advertise the position. Organizations can attract candidates who are qualified, experienced, and genuinely interested in the position if ambiguous descriptions are avoided. Therefore, vacant positions should be advertised in direct, plain, and straight-to-the-point language.

1.2b. Emphasis on the Core Responsibilities and Expectations

Emphasizing core responsibilities and expectations is essential for developing comprehensive job descriptions. Therefore, companies should focus on clearly defining and sharing a job's main duties and performance expectations. This gives candidates a realistic idea of what the job involves. This also allows candidates to assess and make a decision about whether their personal goals and ambitions align with the company's position. Moreover, establishing clear expectations for performance standards, reporting, and culture lays the foundation for mutual respect and accountability between the employer and employee.

2. Effective Sourcing Strategy

The key to successful recruitment is the ability to find talent efficiently, and it requires a broad strategy that is well planned out. These strategies can involve the use of multiple channels, such as online job portals, social media platforms, and networking events. It also involves building and maintaining talent pools by having a database of potential candidates and building relationships with the talent community.

2.1. Utilizing Multiple Channels

Sourcing for potential candidates requires organizations to take a multifaceted approach, that is, make use of online job portals that are industry-specific and general employment placement boards. This approach creates awareness and attraction for a pool of competent candidates. Other channels include social media platforms such as LinkedIn, Facebook, Twitter (now X), and WhatsApp. All of these avenues provide an added layer of soliciting interest from active and passive job seekers. Also, network events and workshops facilitate direct communication with prospective candidates, thereby forging a personal bond and positioning organizations as appealing employers. Here, we focus on three channels, which are online job portals, social media platforms, and networking events.

2.1a. Online Job Portals

Online job portals are a perfect way to find potential candidates. These websites bring job seekers and employers together in one place. Posting jobs on popular portals helps companies reach more applicants and get noticed. More so, these job portals frequently provide options that allow organizations to focus on specific skill sets and qualifications. By focusing on the right candidates, organizations may increase the efficiency of the sourcing process and attract applicants with the necessary skills, experience, and qualifications.

2.1b. Social Media Platforms

Over time, social media platforms have evolved into an important component of modern hiring practices. Social media platforms like LinkedIn, Facebook, X, and WhatsApp have become channels through which organizations reach out to potential employees. Social media provides a more vibrant and engaging platform for promoting the organization's principles, job prospects, and culture. These platforms provide direct contact with passive and active job applicants, that is, people who are receptive to new opportunities and challenges.

2.1c. Networking Events

Networking events are also important sourcing channels for qualified and serious candidates. Organizational executives have direct conversations or interactions with candidates, and most times, the best candidates are lured into taking up offers by multiple organizations. Through network events, organizational representatives establish personal relationships and learn about the motivations, career objectives, and aspirations of job applicants. Networking events are advantageous because they help with recruiting the best talents, have a long-term attraction for recruiting talent on the spot, and save the organization time in the recruiting and interviewing processes.

2.2. Build and Maintain Talent Pools

The two important components here are regularly updating candidates' databases and establishing relationships with potential candidates.

2.2a. Candidate Database

It is essential for organizations to regularly update their candidate database because it will serve as a valuable source for hiring in the future. When new opportunities emerge, the organization goes through its database to find suitable candidates, and if none are found, it outsources the job through other online portals. Through the database, organizations ensure they are not short on talent demands.

2.2b. Establishing Relationships with the Talent Community

Establishing relationships with potential candidates is more than business as usual, as it allows candidates to feel more connected and involved with an organization because they are a part of the talent community. Building relationships with job seekers helps companies connect personally, share industry insights, and show interest in candidates' career growth. This approach boosts the company's reputation and makes candidates more likely to consider working there in the future. Fostering a talent community allows organizations to gain a competitive advantage by attracting the best talents in any industry.

3. Simplifying the Application Process

Attracting and keeping the best talent requires a simplified application process. An easy-to-use application procedure fastens communication, improves applicants' experiences, and reflects positively on an organization's brand image. In this article, we discuss two main components of simplifying the application process: the use of user-friendly application forms and prompt communication.

3.1. User-Friendly Application Forms

The application form is the first point of contact or interaction an organization has with a candidate; therefore, it has to be designed in a manner that simplifies the application process and encourages a high volume of applicants. The user application should be friendly, simple, and without redundant information.

3.1a. Simplifying the Application Process

Simplifying the application process requires reducing the number of required fields and eliminating stages in the application that are unnecessary. It also involves providing clear and coherent instructions on the application process. Lengthy and complex application forms have the potential to irritate applicants and cause them to discontinue the application process. Simplifying the application process makes it easier for candidates to complete the form, which improves the applicants' experience and increases the possibility of attracting a wide range of competent applicants.

3.1b. Reduce Redundant Information

Redundant and unnecessary information in the application process can cause applicants to have a negative perception of an organization. Application forms are supposed to focus on collecting essential information from candidates. For instance, level of experience, qualifications, competencies, and expectations. A clear application form saves time and also demonstrates to applicants that the organization is a committed and dedicated one. Reducing redundant information makes the application process more effective and efficient. It also reduces the risk of applicants' dropouts and improves their overall satisfaction.

3.2. Prompt Communication

Effective communication provides applicants with timely information about their application process. Applicants can feel appreciated and valued when the communication exchange between an organization and them is timely and clear throughout the application and selection process. In order to achieve this, organizations must promptly acknowledge the receipt of applications and provide updates on the hiring process.

3.2a. Acknowledgment of Receipt of Applications

Prompt acknowledgment of the receipts of applications reassures applicants that their applications have been received and have been looking into. This action establishes a good tone and shows the organization's seriousness in the search for the appropriate candidates. It also shows how committed the organization is to its communication efforts.

3.2b. Timely Updates on the Hiring Process

Maintaining applicants' engagement and transparency throughout the hiring process requires timely updates. It eliminates uncertainty and enables candidates to make plans by outlining the anticipated timeframe for each step of the hiring process.

4. Comprehensive Screening and Assessment

People in the workplace often use screening and assessment interchangeably. However, these two words have different meanings. The differences are that screening is used to filter down the number of applicants using certain criteria, and assessment is evaluating further the skill set, qualifications, interests, and hobbies, assessment tests, and interview(s) of an applicant to see if they align with the job vacancy.

Screening in workplace recruitment represents the evaluation of applicants' general and basic qualifications in order to narrow down the number of qualified applicants for the job position. Screening takes time and effort because it helps companies choose the right candidates for a job. It includes an early-stage questionnaire to gather information about an applicant's skills and qualifications. Other criteria used in screening include level and years of experience, salary expectation, and relocation willingness. Although screening is an excellent choice to stream down the volume of applicants, it provides little insight into an applicant's suitability for the vacant position.

On the other hand, assessment takes screening further, meaning that applicants are subjected to test assessments to gain knowledge of their personality traits, competencies, skills, and abilities. Applicants who succeed in the first assessment phase are subject to the second assessment phase, which includes a face-to-face interview with the applicant; this can be virtual or within an organization's environment. The assessment process is systematic and requires applicants to outperform each other for the job position.

However, screening and assessment are critical stages of the recruitment process; as such, the process must be fair, accurate, and in alignment with the vision and goals of the organization. Here, we discuss the structured interviewing process and skills testing and assessment.

4.1. Structured Interviewing Process

Organizations tend to make use of the structured interviewing process because it is consistent and serves as a framework for objective evaluation. In a bid to reduce bias and subjectivity in the recruitment process, the interview questions are predetermined. There are two components to the structured interview process: behavioral and situational questions and the use of multiple interviewers for diverse perspectives.

4.1a. Behavioral and Situational Questions

The purpose of behavioral and situational questions is to elicit specific experiences, both present and past, from applicants and understand how they handled challenges in their previous organization(s). Behavioral and situational questions provide detailed insights of a candidate's problem-solving and communication skills to see if they match the company's needs. Structured interviews have been a reliable way to assess job applicants because they focus on relevant skills and reduce bias.

4.1b. Using Multiple Interviewers

Incorporating multiple interviewers in the assessment process is important for obtaining different perspectives. The interviewers usually consist of people from different departments and levels working in the organization. Diverse interview panels offer different perspectives, which lowers the possibility of personal prejudices and enhances a comprehensive assessment of all applicants for the job. The use of multiple interviewers encourages equality and increases the possibility of finding the most fitting applicants who share the organization's values and can make valuable contributions to different teams in the organization.

4.2. Skills Testing and Assessment

In addition to having multiple interviews, skills testing and assessment offer a concrete and unbiased appraisal of an applicant's competencies and dexterity. Making use of tailored assessment and technology for objective evaluation ensures an accurate prediction of on-the-job performance.

4.2a. Tailored Assessments to Job Requirements

Applicants are evaluated according to their competencies and skills that are relevant for the job through tailored assessments. A one-size-fits-all assessment approach may not be adequate to assess applicants for a vacant position accurately. Therefore, by engaging in a tailored assessment approach, it is possible to provide a more accurate account of the likelihood of the applicant succeeding in the vacant position.

4.2b. Use of Technology for Objective Evaluation

The use of technology is important for achieving objective evaluation during the screening and assessment process. To reduce biases and improve objectivity, it is important to advocate the use of automated tools, artificial intelligence, and data analytics. Technology-enabled assessments can offer a standardized and consistent review procedure that ensures that each applicant is assessed using the same criteria. In addition, technology makes it possible to analyze large datasets quickly and efficiently, thereby empowering hiring organizations to make data-driven choices.

5. Improving Transparent Communication in the Recruitment Process

Transparent communication in the recruitment process extends beyond simply informing candidates. It is important to present an accurate account of the position, business, and culture. It is also important to present a realistic job description. Candidates might not be able to self-select or understand the pros and cons of the position without getting a preview of the job position. The recruiting process, aside from being the selection process for new recruits, presents an opportunity for candidates to determine if the opportunity being presented aligns with their beliefs, values, and goals in life.

Being transparent in communicating the recruitment process allows outsiders, that is, those who are external to the company's affairs, to have a better perception of the company. For instance, in a survey conducted by LinkedIn on job seekers, 94 percent of the total job seekers involved in the survey mentioned that they would accept a job offer if the company was straightforward and transparent about its brand, culture, and goals.

It is important for companies not to raise the expectations of job seekers with false promises. The job opening should provide a clear picture of its expectations, challenges, and opportunities. Open communication helps candidates decide whether to join the company. Throughout the hiring process, updates should be shared regularly, keeping candidates informed about any changes or delays. The status and stages of applications should be made known to candidates. All communications with candidates should be respectful and polite; it indicates to candidates that their interest and time are valued. It also shows the quality of professionalism the company possesses.

225

5.1. Clearly Defining the Recruitment Process

The first step toward ensuring transparency is to provide a concise and comprehensive description of the entire recruitment process. Therefore, it is important to inform each applicant about every stage, the projected timeline, and the evaluation standards. Additionally, it is important to establish realistic expectations for all candidates.

5.1a. Provide Information on Each Stage

Providing information on each stage of the recruitment process is important, as candidates get to experience a transparent and positive process of recruitment. HR scholars emphasize that in order to keep candidates informed and interested, it is critical to be explicit in describing and defining each stage of the recruitment process. Providing information for candidates about the recruitment processes—application review, interviews, and assessments—makes it easier for them to comprehend the schedule and requirements. Fostering a sense of trust and enabling candidates to sufficiently prepare for each step of the recruitment process promotes inclusivity and equality in the process.

5.1b. Set realistic Expectations for Candidates

A significant part of the recruitment process is for companies to set realistic expectations for candidates. Companies should be transparent and make it clear about the job requirements, roles and responsibilities, and possible challenges. Companies should also emphasize the goals, values, and standards of their companies, as it will help candidates make informed decisions about working for the company. Being transparent eliminates fears and misplaced expectations from candidates, and it promotes long-term worker retention and satisfaction.

5.2. Constructive Feedback

Another aspect of transparent communication is providing candidates with timely and constructive feedback. Constructive feedback contributes to the overall experience of candidates in the recruitment process, and it also shows the company's dedication to professional development, regardless of what the outcome is for potential candidates. In this section, we discuss offering feedback to successful and unsuccessful candidates and the focus on development opportunities.

5.2a. Feedback for Successful and Unsuccessful Candidates

Companies should provide feedback to all candidates, irrespective of whether they are successful or unsuccessful in the recruitment process. For instance, giving feedback to unsuccessful candidates helps them understand their strengths and areas where they need to improve their competencies and experiences. Feedback helps show that a company is dedicated to the development and success of candidates and encourages candidates to advance their careers and pursue professionalism.

5.2b. Focus on Development Opportunities

When giving feedback, companies should highlight both strengths and areas for growth. Instead of focusing only on weaknesses, they should emphasize development opportunities and key skills. This approach makes feedback more constructive and encourages candidates to see challenges as chances to learn and improve. Candidates who value growth will appreciate this supportive approach.

6. Emphasis on Diversity, Equality, and Inclusion (DEI)

Diversity, equality, and inclusion (DEI) in the workplace is more than a moral obligation; it is a strategic business decision in this day and age because of the cross-cultural boundaries existing in different nations. The benefits of implementing DEI are enormous; for instance, a report by McKinsey found that companies that were more diverse in teams had a better financial performance of 35 percent than those companies without DEI. The Harvard Business Review mentions that companies with more diverse teams are more innovative, and in a poll carried out by Glassdoor, it was found that 65 percent of job seekers were of the opinion that DEI is important.

Companies that are more open to DEI are more likely to attract the best talents across all industries. Companies that operate with a diverse cultural team tend to have a better understanding of global markets. Therefore, companies need to consider DEI in their recruitment strategies because it is pivotal to achieving the company's objectives and targets. During recruitment, companies should take into consideration ways to implement inclusive practices and promote equal opportunities.

6.1. Implementing Inclusive Practices

Here, the HR team will need to address their personal unconscious biases and ensure that the interview panel is diverse in nature.

6.1a. Address Unconscious Bias among the Hiring Team

Unconscious bias is the automatic and "unintentional" judgment we as people have about others different from us. Unconscious bias is subtle and implicit because it is ingrained in an individual in such a manner that it is considered a norm. It has a strong influence on people's thought processes and actions within the workplace. It is not synonymous with a particular race or gender; everyone tends to have this hidden perception among a group of people because of their race, ethnicity, gender, religious beliefs, and sexual orientation because the mind and emotions have been conditioned to think like that.

The hiring team must address their personal biases before engaging in the interviewing process. Therefore, to help the hiring team, HR can organize DEI trainings to raise awareness and provide strategies to soften unconscious biases. Sometimes, when one's unconscious biases become conscious, it is easier to combat them. Another strategy is the use of blind recruitment strategies, which involve removing identifying information from the résumés in the first screening phase. Blind recruitment could support equitable assessment based on qualifications and expertise instead of demographics.

6.1b. Diverse Interview Panel

Having a diverse interview panel promotes inclusivity in the hiring process. Companies should support the formation of panels with people from different ethnicities, genders, sexual orientations, and religious beliefs. Creating interview panels with diverse members representing different ethnicities, genders, sexual orientations, and religious beliefs helps minimize bias. This ensures candidates are judged on their skills and experience rather than personal differences. A diverse panel promotes fair and objective evaluations. Also, the interview panel will create an environment that eliminates suspicions of bias, discrimination, and nepotism during the hiring process, thereby making potential employees feel seen, heard, and understood.

6.2. The Promotion of Equal Opportunities Is Essential

HR teams can promote equal opportunities for all potential employees by creating a supportive work environment and providing fair and equal compensation for all.

6.2a. Creating a supportive work environment

Creating a supportive work environment encourages a culture of inclusion where all employees feel valued. There should be policies in workplaces that support employees' mental health and work schedules and encourage a work-life balance. Companies should actively promote DEI by offering equitable possibilities for promotion irrespective of employees' differences and diversity.

A supportive work environment should be promoted through mentorship programs, leadership development initiatives, and employee resource groups. Every member of staff should have access to opportunities for growth in a company to increase the chances of selecting the best talents and enhance productivity. By prioritizing a supportive work environment, companies can foster an inclusive workplace where employees can flourish and improve employee retention, satisfaction, and overall success.

6.2b. Fair compensation packages

Equal opportunities should extend beyond the hiring process to an employee's lifecycle in a company. Therefore, it is important to offer fair and transparent compensation packages and plans, which entail carrying out routine pay equity audits to rectify gender, ethnicity, or race wage gaps. Open and honest communication about the criteria for determining salaries is necessary and significant in helping employees build trust and establish strong ties while fulfilling the goals of the company.

10.2. The Don'ts of Recruitment

Source: Designed by Author

1. Neglecting Brand Identity and Image

Organizations should take cognizance of their brand identity and image. A brand identity is what an organization represents; it is what others know it for, and it should be pivotal in the promotion of an organization's entire lifespan. A brand's identity is reflected in its logo, mission, values, and way of operating. It shapes the company's culture and daily practices. Brand image, however, is how outsiders perceive the company, which can vary from person to person. Organizations should strive to make a strong and lasting impression on all applicants. The image an applicant has of an organization could be the attraction he or she has to put their best foot forward in the recruitment and selection process. For instance, working for Tesla, Amazon, and Fortune 100 companies is attractive to applicants because of the perceptions held about working in these places. Organizations should never neglect their brand identity, as this will make it less competitive for talented applicants. The common pitfalls organizations should avoid include avoiding online presence and ignoring employee reviews.

1.1. Avoiding an Online Presence

Every organization should have a dedicated online presence to promote its brand. We live in a world where people are more connected than ever before through digital connectivity. As a result, the best places to recruit candidates are through various online social media platforms that are online. Job applicants research the internet to search for potential vacancies in different organizations that fit their level of qualification and experience. People work remotely and from different time zones; therefore, organizations that do not have an online presence are missing opportunities to attract the best talents. To have a dedicated online presence, organizations need to have an active website and leverage social media platforms for brand visibility.

1.1a. Active and Engaging Website

The ability of an organization to attract prospective prospects may suffer if the organization fails to maintain an active and engaging website. A poorly designed website reflects poorly on the organization's brand identity, and it may deter talented individuals from seeking employment in the organization. Every organization should ensure that their websites offer a wealth of information about the culture, values, career opportunities, and benefits. Content such as blogs, employee testimonials, and videos should be incorporated into the website to show the versatility and richness of the organization.

1.1b. Leverage Social Media for Brand Visibility

Ignoring social media platforms as a tool for brand visibility is an error and a costly mistake for every organization. Social media platforms are a great way to showcase the corporate culture, build brand identity, and interact with prospective employees. These social platforms, such as LinkedIn, Facebook, X, and Instagram, should be used regularly to inform society of upcoming events, accomplishments, social responsibilities, and industry news. Organizations should encourage their followers on their social media platforms by responding to messages and comments and answering their questions promptly to create a positive impression about the organization's brand.

1.2. Ignoring Employee Reviews

Online reviews have become an important source of influence for job applicants looking to take up employment in an organization. Job applicants look to online reviews to decide if they should apply for work in an organization. Therefore, for organizations to protect their reputation, it is necessary to respond to these reviews; if not, it can damage the brand identity and image of the organization. Hence, organizations should engage in monitoring and responding to online reviews and use feedback for continuous improvement.

1.2a. Monitor and Respond to Online Reviews

Disregarding or ignoring employee testimonials on social media or on websites such as Indeed and Glassdoor may harm the reputation of an organization. Before accepting a job offer, applicants often check employee reviews about a company's culture, work ethics, and environment. Organizations should monitor these reviews and respond thoughtfully. Addressing concerns and highlighting workplace benefits demonstrates transparency and commitment to employee well-being and strengthens the company's reputation. Bear in mind that when an organization's reputation is damaged, it is difficult to attract talented applicants.

1.2b. Use Feedback for Continuous Improvement

Feedback from employee reviews, surveys, and interviews should be used to identify areas for further improvement in the recruitment and selection process. The information provided should be used to address concerns raised by employees, improve workplace culture, and strengthen organizational reputation. Demonstrating that an organization listens and is willing to make changes is an attraction for talented and hardworking employees.

2. Rushing the Hiring Process

Organizations should never be in a hurry to hire. Rushing the hiring process will prove to be more costly in the long run. The common pitfalls to avoid in the hiring process are hasty decision-making and skipping reference checks.

2.1. Hasty Decision-Making

During the recruitment process, making hasty decisions can have long-term consequences for the success and culture of an organization. Hasty decisions may lead to recruiting candidates who are mediocre and impact the performance and innovation of the organization. Therefore, organizations must take adequate time to evaluate applicants and prioritize quality over speed.

2.1a. Adequate Time for Evaluation

Companies should take the time to thoroughly assess candidates to ensure the right hire. This includes carefully reviewing résumés, conducting interviews, and testing skills, qualifications, and abilities. It is most likely that organizations that rush through the important steps in the recruitment process could overlook the most important information or become subjective due to personal prejudice. Organizations can make better hiring decisions that align with their values and goals when the hiring process is thoroughly reviewed and assessed.

2.1b. Prioritize Quality over Speed

Prioritizing speed over quality will lead to a poor recruitment process, which will have a long-term impact on the organization's performance. Although organizations may be confronted with the pressure of filling vacancies, it is important that recruiting quality employees be the priority. In order to achieve quality, organizations should set clear selection criteria, conduct thorough interviews, and assess candidates against predetermined standards. Hiring quality over speed is a strategic intent that enables human resource teams to hire the best-performing talents for the overall growth of the organization.

2.2. Skipping Reference Checks

Reference checking is something most employers do in their recruitment and selection processes. Reference checking entails organizations contacting previous employers of a potential applicant, schools to gain knowledge of their qualifications, and supervisors to learn more about their experience, skills, and competencies on the job. While some human resource advocates believe that reference checks are important for validating or refusing a potential applicant, others argue that reference checks go beyond validating an applicant; instead, they are about learning and understanding the strengths and limitations of a candidate on the job.

2.2a. Verifying the Information of Potential Applicants

Organizations that neglect reference checks run the risk of hiring applicants who falsely claim their expertise or skills. Reference checks provide important details about a candidate's character, work ethic, and interpersonal abilities.

It is important to confirm the information that applicants provide during the hiring process. Information such as work history, job titles, responsibilities, skills, and accomplishments. Organizations can verify candidates' statements, find out about any inconsistencies, and gain a deeper understanding of an applicant's suitability for the position. This can be done by getting in touch with the references provided by the applicants or outsourcing it out to organizations that provide reference-checking services online, like Zinc and Xref.

2.2b. Contact Previous Employers

Making contact with former employers is also an important part of the reference-checking process. Previous managers and coworkers can offer valuable insights into a candidate's performance, strengths, and areas for improvement. When employers reach out to past workplaces, they ask specific questions about work quality, punctuality, teamwork, communication, and reliability. Organizations are expected to look out for warning signs or discrepancies in the submitted feedback. The information gathered from multiple sources can be used to make informed decisions about hiring the applicant and mitigate the risk of hiring applicants who do not meet the expectations.

3. Neglecting Legal Compliance

Organizations are exposed to significant risks when they disregard legal compliance during the recruitment process, ranging from lawsuits to reputational harm. Conducting a fair and ethical employment process requires adherence to anti-discriminatory laws and respect for privacy rights.

3.1. Discrimination in Recruitment

Discrimination in recruitment is unethical and illegal. Encouraging diversity and inclusivity in the workplace requires organizations to be aware of and observant of anti-discrimination legislation.

3.1a. Be Aware of Antidiscrimination Laws

There are legal frameworks in the US that prohibit discrimination based on age, gender, color, religion, or handicap. Examples of anti-discriminatory laws include the Civil Rights Act, the Age Discrimination in Employment Act, the Equal Pay Act, the Americans with Disabilities Act, the Immigration Reform and Control Act, and the Fair Employment Act. Therefore, organizations need to remain up-to-date about applicable laws at the federal, state, and industry levels to guarantee that their hiring procedures comply with legal mandates.

3.1b. Avoid Using Biased Language in Job Descriptions

Job descriptions should be written using inclusive language that does not discriminate against or favor people based on protected traits. Adhering to age- or gender-specific requirements or using language that suggests favoritism for specific groups is crucial to upholding anti-discrimination laws.

3.2. Violating Privacy Rights

A key component of ethical recruitment practices is safeguarding the right to privacy of job seekers. Organizations need to get permission before doing background checks and taking precautions to protect the information of job seekers. Here, we discuss two components, which include obtaining consent for background checks and safeguarding candidates' information.

3.2a. Obtaining Consent for Background Checks

Gaining the consent of job seekers is essential for conducting background checks, which are a standard component of the hiring process. To comply with privacy regulations, it is important to notify job seekers about the need for a background check and obtain their consent.

3.2b. Safeguard Candidate Information

After gathering information about candidates, organizations should take care to protect it from disclosure or unauthorized access. Strong encryption, access controls, and cybersecurity safeguards help to protect the confidentiality of candidates and guarantee adherence to privacy laws.

4. Failing to Adapt to Market Trends

Recruitment agencies must acknowledge that talent acquisition is not static; it is ever-evolving. As such, if agencies fail to adapt to market trends, it could hinder the hiring and retention of top talent. Therefore, the common pitfalls to avoid include ignoring industry changes and neglecting employer competitiveness.

4.1. Ignoring Industry Changes

There is a constant change in recruitment agencies that is influenced by ever-evolving technological advancements, changes in candidates' preferences, and shifts in market demands. Recruitment agencies cannot afford to ignore these changes, as they are a precursor for organizations to connect with the right talents. Also, not evolving with changing trends can lead to outdated practices and complete incompetence. Here, we discuss staying informed about recruitment trends and adapting strategies to market demands.

4.1a. Stay Informed about Recruitment Trends

The inability to stay informed about industry changes and recruitment trends can lead organizations to lag behind their competitors. Hence, it is important to keep abreast of new developments in technologies, candidate preferences, and upcoming trends. As a result, recruitment agencies should keep up with changes made to the hiring process, candidate sourcing strategies, and recruitment platforms. Organizations can maintain their competitiveness in the talent market by keeping themselves informed and proactively adjusting their recruitment strategies.

4.1b. Adapting Strategies to Market Dynamics

Market trends, such as shifts in candidate demographics, economic conditions, and industry demands heavily influence recruitment strategies. Ignoring these changes can lead to ineffective hiring and challenges in attracting top talent. Organizations must constantly evaluate the state of the market and adjust their strategies. The process of adjustment could entail refining job descriptions, improving candidate sourcing strategies, and reassessing the selection criteria to meet the changing market demands better.

4.2. Neglecting Employer Competitiveness

In human resources, employer competitiveness is the ability of organizations to attract and retain top talents ahead of their competitors. Therefore, ignoring the factors that give an employer a competitive edge over others may lead to a scarcity of skilled workers and make it difficult to attract top talents. To gain employer competitiveness, it will require a regular review and adjustment of compensation packages and the assessment and improvement of employee benefits.

4.2a Regular Review and Adjustment of Compensation Packages

One of the biggest ways that organizations can lose top talent is when they fail to review and adjust compensation packages regularly. Offering competitive pay and benefits is important in a competitive labor market to attract top talents. Organizations must carry out regular wage benchmarking in order to maintain the competitiveness of their compensation packages relative to their industry and geographical location. Hence, to improve employer competitiveness, there is a need to take into account bonuses, nonmonetary benefits, and performance-based incentives.

4.2b. Improving Employee Benefits

Organizations need to evaluate and enhance their benefit programs to avoid competition for top talents. Organizations need to ensure that employee benefits are up-to-date with changing employee expectations by regularly assessing them. Offering flexible work schedules, wellness initiatives, chances for professional growth, or extra benefits like assistance with childcare or student loan repayment are a few ways to achieve this. Organizations may attract more people and build their employer brand by improving their employee benefit packages.

5. Relying Solely on Technology

Technology has no doubt been revolutionary in the recruitment and selection process; however, depending solely on it can lead to monolithic interactions and omissions. Some of the common pitfalls to avoid include automated decision-making and a lack of personalization.

5.1. Automated Decision-Making

Here we discuss how to balance technology with human judgment and the use of artificial intelligence (AI) ethically and authentically.

5.1a. Balancing Technology with Human Judgment

Automated decision-making tools help in no small measure to improve the recruitment and selection process; however, they cannot predict human judgment or intentions. Hence, it's important to balance technology with human judgment. Technology should be used efficiently to screen résumés and filter applications based on set criteria. Despite technological benefits, human judgment is crucial in determining soft skills, cultural fits, and other qualitative aspects that algorithms may regulate. Hence, organizations can make better recruitment and selection decisions that are consistent with their goals and values by integrating human judgment into the decision-making process.

5.1b. Using AI Ethically and Authentically

AI should be used in the recruiting process ethically and authentically. It is important to train AI systems on objective data and to continuously check their accuracy and fairness. To preserve candidates' confidence and trust, openness about the usage of AI in the recruitment process is important. Employing practices, data collection practices and the use of AI in hiring should all be transparent to employees. Furthermore, candidates should be able to decide whether to submit their assessments for human review or to forego AI-powered evaluations.

5.2. Lack of Personalization

Lack of personalization can hinder interactions with candidates or job seekers despite the manner in which technology simplifies the hiring process. Candidates value and appreciate a personalized approach that recognizes their skills, competencies, and attributes. Here we discuss personalized communication with candidates and avoiding generic automated responses.

5.2a. Personalized Communication with Candidates

Candidates may feel detached from the recruitment process if there is no personal communication. Although technology makes automated communication possible, it is important to ensure that each candidate receives a tailored message during the recruitment process. Personalized communication is a sign of sincere interest in candidates' distinctive qualifications, competencies, skills, and experiences. Recruitment agencies should utilize information acquired during the hiring process, such as specific job preferences or past interactions, to personalize communication and demonstrate to job seekers the importance of their unique requirements and interests.

5.2b. Avoiding Generic Automated Responses

When job seekers receive generic, automated responses, it makes them feel undervalued and disconnected from the recruitment process. Make an effort to create thoughtful, individualized responses to application materials, feedback, and questions from candidates instead of depending on premade templates. Recruitment agencies should endeavor to refer to candidates by their names, recognize their qualifications or experiences, and give pertinent information based on their questions or concerns. Personalized responses are a demonstration that the time and efforts of candidates are appreciated; this can leave a positive experience.

10.3. Conclusion

In this chapter, all the important dos and don'ts of recruitment have been extensively covered. The goal is to ensure that organizations are well-equipped with the knowledge and strategies needed to build a successful and ethically responsible recruitment practice. The important dos include detailed job analysis, effective sourcing strategies, a streamlined application process, thorough screening and assessment, open communication, and a focus on diversity and inclusion. While the don'ts of recruitment encompass neglecting employer branding, rushing the recruitment process, overlooking candidate experiences, competencies, and skills, and ignoring company brand.

Technology breakthroughs, the dynamic nature of the labor market, and changing applicant expectations highlight how important it is to keep improving recruitment procedures. The important components of a dynamic recruitment approach include adapting to market trends, staying abreast of industry changes, and regularly reviewing and adjusting strategies. Organizations that place a high priority on continuous development place themselves in a position to attract top talents, handle challenges head-on, and stay ahead of the competition in the rapidly changing talent acquisition landscape.

Developing an effective recruitment strategy calls for a comprehensive and strategic approach, not just following a list of dos and don'ts. It involves understanding the company's needs, building a strong reputation as an employer, and treating candidates with respect. Combining technology with human judgment creates a fair, efficient hiring process that aligns with the company's values. Through the implementation of diversity and inclusion strategies, adherence to regulatory requirements, and ongoing improvement of recruitment procedures, organizations may build a framework for talent acquisition that not only fulfills their short-term requirements but also fosters long-term success.

In conclusion, a successful recruitment strategy should be dynamic and constantly evolving, marked by adaptability, transparency, and commitment to quality. Embracing the lessons from the dos and don'ts provided in this chapter will surely help organizations establish a strong and successful recruitment strategy as they negotiate the complexity of the talent market.

References

Adamovic, M. (2022). When ethnic discrimination in recruitment is likely to occur and how to reduce it: applying a contingency perspective to review résumé studies. *Human Resource Management Review*, *32*(2), 100832.

Affum-Osei, E., and Chan, D. K. (2024). Job search in a difficult labour market: linking goal orientation to job search strategies and outcomes with the moderating role of self-control. *Current Psychology*, *43*(4), 2947–2964.

Agarwal, P. (2020). *Sway: Unravelling unconscious bias.* Bloomsbury Publishing.

Ahmad, R., Nawaz, M. R., and Ishaq, M. I. (2023). Social exchange theory: Systematic review and future directions. *Frontiers in Psychology*, *13*, 1015921.

Al-dalahmeh, M., Khalaf, R., and Obeidat, B. (2018). The effect of employee engagement on organizational performance via the mediating role of job satisfaction: The case of IT employees in the Jordanian banking sector. *Modern Applied Science*, *12*(6), 17–43.

Alt, D., Kapshuk, Y., and Dekel, H. (2023). Promoting perceived creativity and innovative behavior: Benefits of future problem-solving programs for higher education students. *Thinking Skills and Creativity*, *47*, 101201.

Arjoon, S. (2006). Striking a balance between rules and principles-based approaches for effective governance: A risk-based approach. *Journal of Business Ethics*, *68*(1), 53–82.

Autor, D. (2022). *The labor market impacts of technological change: From unbridled enthusiasm to qualified optimism to vast uncertainty* (No. w30074). National Bureau of Economic Research.

Ardi, A., Cahyadi, H., Meilani, Y. F., and Pramono, R. (2024). Talent attraction through flexible work anytime from anywhere. *Journal of Infrastructure, Policy and Development, 8*(3).

Ashforth, B. K., and Saks, A. M. (1996). Socialization tactics: Longitudinal effects on newcomer adjustment. *Academy of Management Journal, 39*(1), 149–178.

Aycan, Z., Al-Hamadi, A. B., Davis, A., and Budhwar, P. (2007). Cultural orientations and preferences for HRM policies and practices: the case of Oman. *The international journal of human resource management, 18*(1), 11–32.

Baert, P., and Da Silva, F. C. (2010). *Social theory in the twentieth century and beyond.* Polity.

Bartlett, K. T., Rhode, D. L., Grossman, J. L., Brake, D. L., and Cooper, F. R. (2022). *Gender and Law: Theory, Doctrine, Commentary [Connected EBook].* Aspen Publishing.

Bakker, A. B., and Leiter, M. P. (2010). *Work engagement: A handbook of essential theory and research.* Psychology Press.

Barak, M. E. M. (2022). *Managing diversity: Toward a globally inclusive workplace.* Sage Publications.

Bashir, B., and Gani, A. (2020). Testing the effects of job satisfaction on organizational commitment. *Journal of Management Development, 39*(4), 525–542.

Bauer, T. N., and Erdogan, B. (2019). *Organizational socialization: The effective onboarding of new employees.* Routledge.

———. (2021). The impact of organizational socialization tactics on newcomer adjustment. *Journal of Applied Psychology,* 106(5), 615–628.

Bayona, J. A., Caballer, A., and Peiró, J. M. (2020). The relationship between knowledge characteristics' fit and job satisfaction and job performance: The mediating role of work engagement. *Sustainability, 12*(6), 2336.

Beal III, L., Stavros, J. M., and Cole, M. L. (2013). Effect of psychological capital and resistance to change on organisational citizenship behaviour. *SA Journal of Industrial Psychology*, *39*(2), 1–11.

Ben-Gal, H. C. (2020). *Fit in the Future of Work 2050: Towards a Person-Skills Fit Perspective*. SSRN.

Bergelson, I., Tracy, C., and Takacs, E. (2022). Best practices for reducing bias in the interview process. *Current urology reports*, *23*(11), 319–325.

Bernhardt, C. (2022). *Nonverbal Communication in Recruiting: How to identify suitable applicants and attract them to your company*. Springer Nature.

Bhargava, V. R., and Assadi, P. (2023). Hiring, Algorithms, and Choice: Why Interviews Still Matter. *Business Ethics Quarterly*, 1–30.

Bilan, Y., Mishchuk, H., Roshchyk, I., and Joshi, O. (2020). Hiring and retaining skilled employees in SMEs: problems in human resource practices and links with organizational success. *Business: Theory and Practice*, *21*(2), 780–791.

Boselie, P. (2014). *Ebook: Strategic human resource management: A balanced approach*. McGraw-Hill.

Boswell, W. R., Payne, S. C., and Bowman-Callaway, C. E. (2024). Recruiting employed job candidates. In *Essentials of Employee Recruitment* (pp. 171–193). Routledge.

Breaugh, J. A. (2024). A history of recruitment research. In *Essentials of Employee Recruitment* (pp. 13–35). Routledge.

Breaugh, J. A., and Starke, M. (2000). Research on employee recruitment: So many studies, so many remaining questions. *Journal of Management*, *26*(3), 405–434.

Brown, C., Jones, D., and Miller, E. (2019). Communication transparency in recruitment agencies. *Journal of Organizational Communication*, 15(3), 120–135.

———. (2020). *Specialisation and expertise in recruitment agencies. Journal of Career Development*, 25(2), 80–95.

———. (2021). *Fit with career aspirations: Understanding job seekers' long-term goals. Journal of Career Development*, 32(2), 80–95.

Brynjolfsson, E., and McAfee, A. (2014). *The second machine age: Work, progress, and prosperity in a time of brilliant technologies*. WW Norton and Company.

Buettner, R. (2017). Getting a job via career-oriented social networking markets. *Electronic Markets, 27*(4), 371–385.

Buil, I., Catalán, S., and Martínez, E. (2020). Understanding applicants' reactions to gamified recruitment. *Journal of Business Research, 110,* 41–50.

Bunt, D., van Kessel, R., Hoekstra, R. A., Czabanowska, K., Brayne, C., Baron-Cohen, S., and Roman-Urrestarazu, A. (2020). Quotas, and anti-discrimination policies relating to autism in the EU: scoping review and policy mapping in Germany, France, Netherlands, United Kingdom, Slovakia, Poland, and Romania. *Autism Research, 13*(8), 1397–1417.

Busque-Carrier, M., Ratelle, C. F., and Le Corff, Y. (2022). Work values and job satisfaction: The mediating role of basic psychological needs at work. *Journal of career development, 49*(6), 1386–1401.

Bustaman, H. A., Mohd nor, M. N., Taha, A. Z., and Zakaria, M. (2020). Job seeker attraction to organizational justice mediated by organizational reputation. *Cogent Psychology, 7*(1), 1816255.

Cable, D. M., and Vermeulen, F. (2023). Organizational socialization and employee engagement: A longitudinal study. *Journal of Organizational Behavior, 44*(2), 287–303.

Caligiuri, P. (2012). *Cultural agility: Building a pipeline of successful global professionals*. John Wiley and Sons.

Carey, H., Florisson, R., and Giles, L. (2019). Skills, talent, and diversity in the creative industries. *Creative Industries Policy and Evidence Centre.*

Carlson, R., Duff, M. C., Flake, D. F., and Bales, R. A. (2023). *Employment law.* Aspen Publishing.

Cascio, W. F. (2019). Training trends: Macro, micro, and policy issues. *Human Resource Management Review, 29*(2), 284–297.

Cascio, W. F., and Aguinis, H. (2008). 3 Staffing twenty-first-century organizations. *Academy of Management Annals, 2*(1), 133–165.

Cascio, W. F., and Aguinis, H. (2005). Applied psychology in human resource management (6th ed.). Pearson/Prentice Hall.

Chandan, J. S. (2009). *Organizational behaviour.* Vikas Publishing House.

Chapman, D. S., Uggerslev, K. L., Carroll, S. A., Piasentin, K. A., and Jones, D. A. (2018). Applicant attraction to organizations and job choice: A meta-analytic review of the correlates of recruiting outcomes. *Journal of Applied Psychology,* 103(6), 613–634. https://doi.org/10.1037/apl0000286.

Chauhan, R. S. (2022). Unstructured interviews: are they really all that bad?. *Human Resource Development International, 25*(4), 474–487.

Chavadi, C. A., Sirothiya, M., and MR, V. (2022). Mediating role of job satisfaction on turnover intentions and job mismatch among millennial employees in Bengaluru. *Business Perspectives and Research, 10*(1), 79–100.

Cherian, J., Gaikar, V., Paul, R., and Pech, R. (2021). Corporate culture and its impact on employees' attitude, performance, productivity, and behavior: An investigative analysis from selected organizations of the United Arab Emirates (UAE). *Journal of Open Innovation: Technology, Market, and Complexity, 7*(1), 45.

Chhabra, B. (2015). Person–job fit: Mediating role of job satisfaction and organizational commitment. *The Indian Journal of Industrial Relations*, 638–651.

Chowdhury, S., Budhwar, P., Dey, P. K., Joel-Edgar, S., and Abadie, A. (2022). AI-employee collaboration and business performance: Integrating knowledge-based view, socio-technical systems and organisational socialisation framework. *Journal of Business Research*, *144*, 31–49.

Clampitt, P. G. (2016). *Communicating for Managerial Effectiveness: Challenges| Strategies| Solutions*. Sage Publications.

Coetzee, M. (2021). Career wellbeing and career agility as coping attributes in the modern career space. In *Agile Coping in the Digital Workplace: Emerging Issues for Research and Practice* (pp. 35–51). Cham: Springer International Publishing.

Compton, R. L. (2009). *Effective recruitment and selection practices*. CCH Australia Limited.

Dale, G. (2020). *Flexible working: How to implement flexibility in the workplace to improve employee and business performance*. Kogan Page Publishers.

Davis, R., and Aspray, W. (2020). *The role of recruitment agencies in accessing hidden job opportunities*. *Journal of Employment Opportunities*, *25*(3), 45-62.

Davies, J., Heasman, B., Livesey, A., Walker, A., Pellicano, E., and Remington, A. (2023). Access to employment: A comparison of autistic, neurodivergent and neurotypical adults' experiences of hiring processes in the United Kingdom. *Autism*, *27*(6), 1746–1763.

De Bie, A., Marquis, E., Cook-Sather, A., and Luqueño, L. (2023). *Promoting equity and justice through pedagogical partnership*. Taylor and Francis.

DeCenzo, D. A., Robbins, S. P., and Verhulst, S. L. (2016). *Fundamentals of human resource management*. John Wiley and Sons.

Diana, I. N., Supriyanto, A. S., Ekowati, V. M., and Ertanto, A. H. (2021). Factor influencing employee performance: The role of organizational culture. *The Journal of Asian Finance, Economics and Business, 8*(2), 545–553.

Doxey, C. H. (2021). *The controller's Toolkit.* John Wiley and Sons.

Dunn, M. B., and Woodruff, T. (2017). Recruiting discrimination: A meta-analysis of field experiments. *Journal of Economic Behavior and Organization, 139,* 39–56. https://doi.org/10.1016/j.jebo.2017.04.016.

Edwards, J. R. (1991). *Person-job fit: A conceptual integration, literature review, and methodological critique.* John Wiley and Sons.

Ellis, J. K. (2014). *Competency-based hiring interviews and university teaching performance.* Barry University.

Ely, R. J., and Thomas, D. A. (2001). Cultural diversity at work: The effects of diversity perspectives on work group processes and outcomes. *Administrative science quarterly, 46*(2), 229–273.

Fein, M. (2012). *Test development: Fundamentals for certification and evaluation.* Association for Talent Development.

Fisher, C. D. (2003). Why do lay people believe that satisfaction and performance are correlated? Possible sources of a common-sense theory. *Journal of Organizational Behavior: The International Journal of Industrial, Occupational and Organizational Psychology and Behavior, 24*(6), 753–777.

Fossen, F. M., and Sorgner, A. (2022). New digital technologies and heterogeneous wage and employment dynamics in the United States: Evidence from individual-level data. *Technological Forecasting and Social Change, 175,* 121381.

Frank, F. D., and Taylor, C. R. (2004). Talent management: Trends that will shape the future. *Human Resource Planning, 27*(1).

Freiha, S. S., and Sassine, M. E. (2023). The impact of organisational justice on workplace outcomes: mediating role of social exchange construct. *EuroMed Journal of Management, 5*(2), 130–150.

Gandini, A. (2016). Digital work: Self-branding and social capital in the freelance knowledge economy. *Marketing theory, 16*(1), 123–141.

Gara, G. L., and La Porte, J. M. (2020). Processes of building trust in organizations: internal communication, management, and recruiting. *Church, Communication and Culture, 5*(3), 298–319.

Garcia, M., and Martinez, J. (2020). *The role of feedback and communication in job seeker satisfaction.* Journal of Organizational Communication, 28(3), 150–165.

Garcia, M., and Martinez, J. (2021). *Cultural and organizational fit in job matches.* Journal of Organizational Behavior, 25(4), 210–225.

Gergen, K. J. (2021). Social exchange theory in a world of transient facts. In *Behavioral theory in sociology* (pp. 91–114). Routledge.

Gerson, K., and Damaske, S. (2020). *The science and art of interviewing.* Oxford University Press.

Gilch, P. M., and Sieweke, J. (2021). Recruiting digital talent: The strategic role of recruitment in organisations' digital transformation. *German Journal of Human Resource Management, 35*(1), 53–82.

Gregory, B. T., Harris, S. G., Armenakis, A. A., and Shook, C. L. (2009). Organizational culture and effectiveness: A study of values, attitudes, and organizational outcomes. *Journal of Business Research, 62*(7), 673–679.

Hamid, S. N. A., and Yahya, K. K. (2016). Mediating role of work engagement on the relationship between person-job fit and employees' retention: Evidence from semiconductor companies in the northern region of Malaysia. *International Review of Management and Marketing, 6*(7), 187–194.

Haidar, J., and Keune, M. (2021). Introduction: Work and labour relations in global platform capitalism. In *Work and labour relations in global platform capitalism* (pp. 1–27). Edward Elgar Publishing.

Hayter, S. (2015). Unions and collective bargaining. *Labour Markets, Institutions and Inequality*, 95–122.

Herkes, J., Churruca, K., Ellis, L. A., Pomare, C., and Braithwaite, J. (2019). How people fit in at work: Systematic review of the association between person–organisation and person–group fit with staff outcomes in healthcare. *BMJ open*, *9*(5), e026266.

Hirst, G., Curtis, S., Nielsen, I., Smyth, R., Newman, A., and Xiao, N. (2023). Refugee recruitment and workplace integration: An opportunity for human resource management scholarship and impact. *Human Resource Management Journal*, *33*(4), 783–805.

Horn, S., Lecomte, P., and Tietze, S. (Eds.). (2020). *Managing multilingual workplaces: Methodological, empirical and pedagogic perspectives*. Routledge.

Hosain, M. S., and Mamun, A. M. A. (2023). The roles of LinkedIn-based skill endorsements and LinkedIn-based hiring recommendations on hiring preferences: evidence from Bangladeshi employers. *Management Matters*, *20*(2), 169–184.

Hunkenschroer, A. L., and Luetge, C. (2022). Ethics of AI-enabled recruiting and selection: A review and research agenda. *Journal of Business Ethics*, *178*(4), 977–1007.

Iacoboni, M. (2009). *Mirroring people: The new science of how we connect with others*. Farrar, Straus and Giroux.

Johennesse, L. A. C., and Chou, T. K. (2017). Employee Perceptions of Talent Management Effectiveness on Retention. *Global Business and Management Research*, *9*(3).

Johnson, A., and Martinez, J. (2019). *Demonstrating adaptability and flexibility in recruitment agencies. Journal of Diversity in the Workplace*, *20*(2), 80–95.

————. (2019). *Long-term viability and stability in job matches.* *Journal of Employment Opportunities*, 40(2), 90–105.

Johnson, A., and Smith, B. (2021). Personalized job matching services: A key expectation from recruitment agencies. *Journal of Career Development*, 27(2), 78–93.

Johnston, H., and Land-Kazlauskas, C. (2018). *Organizing on-demand representation, voice, and collective bargaining in the gig economy* (No. 994981993502676). International Labour Organization.

Jones, L., and Johnson, M. (2021). *The efficiency of recruitment agencies in job placement. Journal of Employment Studies*, 30(4), 112–129.

Jones, M., and Shelton, M. (2011). *Developing your portfolio-Enhancing your learning and showing your stuff: A Guide for the early childhood student or professional.* Routledge.

Kaur, N., and Kang, L. S. (2021). Person-organisation fit, person-job fit and organisational citizenship behaviour: An examination of the mediating role of job satisfaction. *IIMB Management Review, 33*(4), 347–359.

Keaveney, J., and Woodcock, B. (2017). *Graduate CVs and Covering Letters.* Bloomsbury Publishing.

Kedharnath, U., Shore, L. M., and Dulebohn, J. H. (2020). Organizational trust among job seekers: The role of information-seeking and reciprocation wariness. *International Journal of Selection and Assessment, 28*(3), 351–363.

Kim, H., and Lee, J. (2021). Ethical and fair practices in recruitment agencies. *Journal of Business Ethics*, 40(2), 180–195.

Kooij, D. T., and Boon, C. (2018). Perceptions of HR practices, person–organisation fit, and affective commitment: The moderating role of career stage. *Human Resource Management Journal, 28*(1), 61–75.

Krings, F., Gioaba, I., Kaufmann, M., Sczesny, S., and Zebrowitz, L. (2021). Older and Younger Job Seekers' Impression Management on LinkedIn. *Journal of personnel psychology*.

Kristof-Brown, A. L., Zimmerman, R. D., and Johnson, E. C. (2005). Consequences OF INDIVIDUALS'FIT at Work: A Meta–Analysis of Person–Job, Person–Organization, Person–Group, and person–Person-Person-Supervisor Fit. *Personnel psychology, 58*(2), 281–342.

Kroll, E., Veit, S., and Ziegler, M. (2021). The discriminatory potential of modern recruitment trends—A mixed-method study from Germany. *Frontiers in Psychology, 12*, 634376.

LeDoux, A. M., and Ramsay, R. S. (2016). The importance of training for ethics and social responsibility in the selection interview. In J. D. Outtz (Ed.), Adverse impact: Implications for organizational staffing and high-stakes selection (pp. 263–286). Routledge.

Lee, H. R., Ahn, Y. Y., and Han, I. (2011). The effect of privacy concerns on user acceptance of services. *Journal of the American Society for Information Science and Technology, 62*(7), 1303–1316.

Lee, H., and Kim, S. (2018). *Networking opportunities provided by recruitment agencies. Journal of Professional Networking*, 12(1), 30–45.

———. (2019). *Geographical coverage and reach of recruitment agencies. Journal of Employment Opportunities*, 30(1), 45–60.

———. (2020). *Importance of follow-up after interviews and job offers. Journal of Career Development*, 30(1), 45–60.

———. (2020). *Opportunities for learning and development in job matches. Journal of Human Resources Management*, 35(1), 45–60.

Lee, S. B., and Suh, T. (2020). Internal audience strikes back from the outside: Emotionally exhausted employees' negative word-of-mouth as the active brand-oriented deviance. *Journal of Product and Brand Management, 29*(7), 863–876.

Lengnick-Hall, M. L., Beck, T. E., and Lengnick-Hall, C. A. (2019). Developing a capacity for organizational resilience through strategic human resource management. *Human Resource Management Review*, 29(2), 126–138. https://doi.org/10.1016/j.hrmr.2018.07.002.

Lenton, A. (2021). *Investigating the theory and practice of inclusive talent management* (Doctoral dissertation, Kingston University).

Leutner, F., Akhtar, R., and Chamorro-Premuzic, T. (2022). Digital Interviews. In *The Future of Recruitment* (pp. 51–87). Emerald Publishing Limited.

Levine, A. G. (2015). *Networking for nerds: find, access, and land hidden game-changing career opportunities everywhere.* John Wiley and Sons.

Ling, F. Y. Y., Ning, Y., Chang, Y. H., and Zhang, Z. (2018). Human resource management practices to improve project managers' job satisfaction. *Engineering, construction and architectural management*, 25(5), 654–669.

Liu, S., Huang, J. L., and Wang, M. (2014). Effectiveness of job search interventions: a meta-analytic review. *Psychological bulletin*, 140(4), 1009.

Locke, E. A. (1976). Job satisfaction and job performance: A theoretical analysis. *Organizational behavior and human performance*, 5(5), 484–500.

Lu, H. (2021). Electronic portfolios in higher education: A review of the literature. *European Journal of Education and Pedagogy*, 2(3), 96–101.

Lu, A. J., and Dillahunt, T. R. (2021). Uncovering the promises and challenges of social media use in the low-wage labor market: insights from employers. In *Proceedings of the 2021 CHI Conference on Human Factors in Computing Systems* (pp. 1–13).

Lu, A. J., Gilhool, A., Hsiao, J. C. Y., and Dillahunt, T. R. (2022). Emotional Labor in Everyday Resilience: Class-based Experiences of

Navigating Unemployment Amid the COVID-19 Pandemic in the US. *Proceedings of the ACM on Human-Computer Interaction*, 6(CSCW2), 1–27.

Mahapatro, B. (2021). *Human resource management*. New Age International (P) Ltd.

McCarthy, J. M., and Cheng, B. H. (2018). Through the looking glass: Employment interviews from the lens of job candidates. *U. Klehe, and van Hooft (Eds.), The Oxford handbook of job loss and job search*, 329–357.

McDonnell, A., and Wiblen, S. (2020). *Talent management: A research overview*. Routledge.

McKinsey and Company (2022). *Race in the workplace: the frontline experience*. Retrieved March 2024 from: https://www.mckinsey.com/featured-insights/diversity-and-inclusion/race-in-the-workplace-the-frontline-experience.

Mensah, J. K., and Bawole, J. N. (2020). Person–job fit matters in parastatal institutions: Testing the mediating effect of person–job fit in the relationship between talent management and employee outcomes. *International Review of Administrative Sciences*, 86(3), 479–495.

Michelson, E., and Mandell, A. (2023). *Portfolio development and the assessment of prior learning: Perspectives, models and practices*. Taylor and Francis.

Migdadi, M. M. (2020). Knowledge management, customer relationship management, and innovation capabilities. *Journal of Business and Industrial Marketing*, 36(1), 111–124.

Miller, A. (2022). *Cybersecurity Career Guide*. Simon and Schuster.

Mohammad, T., Darwish, T. K., Singh, S., and Khassawneh, O. (2021). Human resource management and organisational performance: The mediating role of social exchange. *European Management Review*, 18(1), 125–136.

Moore, S., Onaran, O., Guschanski, A., Antunes, B., and Symon, G. (2019). The resilience of collective bargaining–a renewed logic for joint regulation?. *Employee Relations: The International Journal, 41*(2), 279–295.

Morgan, J. (2017). *The employee experience advantage: How to win the war for talent by giving employees the workspaces they want, the tools they need, and a culture they can celebrate.* John Wiley and Sons.

Mutuku, C. K., and Mathooko, P. (2014). Effects of organizational communication on employee motivation: A case study of Nokia Siemens Networks Kenya. *International Journal of Social Sciences and Project Planning Management, 1*(3), 28–62.

Nankervis, A., Baird, M., Coffey, J., and Shields, J. (2019). *Human resource management.* Cengage, AU.

Nasifoglu Elidemir, S., Ozturen, A., and Bayighomog, S. W. (2020). Innovative behaviors, employee creativity, and sustainable competitive advantage: A moderated mediation. *Sustainability, 12*(8), 3295.

Naz, S., Li, C., Nisar, Q. A., Khan, M. A. S., Ahmad, N., and Anwar, F. (2020). A study in the relationship between supportive work environment and employee retention: Role of organizational commitment and person–organization fit as mediators. *Sage Open, 10*(2), 2158244020924694.

Nayak, B. C., Nayak, G. K., and Jena, D. (2020). Social recognition and employee engagement: The effect of social media in organizations. *International Journal of Engineering Business Management, 12*, 1847979020975109.

Nikolaou, I., and Georgiou, K. (2018). Fairness reactions to the employment interview. *Journal of Work and Organizational Psychology, 34*(2), 103–111.

Noon, M., and Ogbonna, E. (2021). Controlling management to deliver diversity and inclusion: Prospects and limits. *Human Resource Management Journal, 31*(3), 619–638.

Okolie, U. C., Nwajiuba, C. A., Binuomote, M. O., Ehiobuche, C., Igu, N. C. N., and Ajoke, O. S. (2020). Career training with mentoring programs in higher education: facilitating career development and employability of graduates. *Education+ Training, 62*(3), 214–234.

Ormerod, R. (2020). The history and ideas of sociological functionalism: Talcott Parsons, modern sociological theory, and the relevance for OR. *Journal of the Operational Research Society, 71*(12), 1873–1899.

O'Rourke, D. (2003). Outsourcing regulation: Analyzing nongovernmental systems of labor standards and monitoring. *Policy Studies Journal, 31*(1), 1–29.

Paillé, P. (2022). Managing green recruitment for attracting pro-environmental job seekers: Toward a conceptual model of "Handicap" principle. In *Sustainable human resource management* (pp. 57–89). River Publishers.

Panayotakis, C. (2014). Capitalism, Meritocracy, and Social Stratification: A Radical Reformulation of the D avis-M oore Thesis. *American Journal of Economics and Sociology, 73*(1), 126–150.

Patel, R., and Williams, S. (2020). Timeliness and responsiveness in recruitment agency interactions. *Journal of Employment Practices, 35*(4), 210–225.

———. (2021). *Comprehensive services offered by recruitment agencies. Journal of Human Resources Management, 18*(4), 210–225.

———. (2022). *Foundational principles of transparent communication in recruitment agencies. Journal of Organizational Communication,* 30(4), 210–225.

Pattnaik, S., and Padhi, M. (2021). Challenges in assessment centres: Lessons from experience. *Management and Labour Studies, 46*(3), 313–336.

Paschina, S. (2023). Trust in Management and Work Flexibility: A Quantitative Investigation of Modern Work Dynamics and their Impact on Organizational Performance. *European Research Studies Journal, 26*(3), 184–196.

Phillips, C., Esterman, A., and Kenny, A. (2015). The theory of organisational socialisation and its potential for improving transition experiences for new graduate nurses. *Nurse education today, 35*(1), 118–124.

Ployhart, R. E., and Moliterno, T. P. (2011). Emergence of the human capital resource: A multilevel model. *Academy of Management Review, 36*(1), 127–150.

Poister, T. H. (2008). *Measuring performance in public and nonprofit organizations.* John Wiley and Sons.

Polat, H. H. (2019). Impact of Cultural Dimensions to Individualism, and Collectivism Dimension. *Journal of Business and Economics, ISSN,* 2155–7950.

PwC (2020). *The future of Remote Work: Global PwC Survey Outputs.* Retrieved March 2024 from: file:///pwc-the-future-of-remote-work-global-pwc-survey-outputs.pdf.

Rankine, D., and Giberti, M. (2020). *Reinventing live: The always-on future of events.* Anthem Press.

Robinson, E., and Nolis, J. (2020). *Build a career in data science.* Manning Publications.

Rode, J. C., Huang, X., and Schroeder, R. G. (2022). Human resources practices and continuous improvement and learning across cultures. *Journal of International Management, 28*(4), 100972.

Schmid, G. (2016). Equality and Efficiency in the Labor Market: Toward a Socioeconomic Theory of Cooperation. In *Labor Market*

Institutions in Europe: A Socioeconomic Evaluation of Performance (pp. 243-279). Routledge.

Schmitt, N., and Chan, D. (1998). *Personnel selection: A theoretical approach.* Sage.

Scott, J., and Marshall, G. (Eds.). (2009). *A dictionary of sociology.* Oxford University Press, USA.

Segre, S. (2016). *Contemporary sociological thinkers and theories.* Routledge.

Smith, J., Brown, A., and Johnson, T. (2019). *Expertise and guidance: The role of recruitment agencies in job seekers' career development. Journal of Career Counseling,* 15(2), 87–104.

Smith, A., and Johnson, B. (2021). *Credibility and reputation of recruitment agencies: A key consideration for job seekers. Journal of Employment Studies,* 40(3), 150–165.

———. (2022). *Accessibility and responsiveness in recruitment agencies: Impact on job seeker satisfaction. Journal of Employment Studies,* 45(2), 80–95.

Smith, W., and Lewis, M. (2022). *Both/and thinking: Embracing creative tensions to solve your toughest problems.* Harvard Business Press.

Solove, D. J., and Schwartz, P. M. (2020). *Information privacy law.* Aspen Publishing.

Fairholm, G. W. (1994). *Leadership and the culture of trust.* Bloomsbury Publishing USA.

Southwick, D. A., Tsay, C. J., and Duckworth, A. L. (2019). Grit at work. *Research in Organizational Behavior, 39,* 100126.

Sovacool, B. K., Axsen, J., and Sorrell, S. (2018). Promoting novelty, rigor, and style in energy social science: Towards codes of practice for appropriate methods and research design. *Energy research and social science, 45,* 12–42.

Stephens, N. M., Rivera, L. A., and Townsend, S. S. (2020). What works to increase diversity? A multi-level approach. *Research in Organizational Behavior, 39*, 1–51.

Stone, D. L., Stone-Romero, E. F., and Lukaszewski, K. M. (2007). The impact of cultural values on the acceptance and effectiveness of human resource management policies and practices. *Human resource management review, 17*(2), 152–165.

Sugiarti, E. (2022). The Influence of Training, Work Environment, and Career Development on Work Motivation That Has an Impact on Employee Performance at PT. Suryamas Elsindo Primatama in West Jakarta. *International Journal of Artificial Intelligence Research, 6*(1), 1–11.

Sundstrup, E., Seeberg, K. G. V., Bengtsen, E., and Andersen, L. L. (2020). A systematic review of workplace interventions to rehabilitate musculoskeletal disorders among employees with physical demanding work. *Journal of occupational rehabilitation, 30*(4), 588–612.

Thomas, D. A, and Gabarro, J. J. (1999). *Breaking through: The making of minority executives in corporate America*. Boston: Harvard Business School Press.

Thompson, N. (2020). *Anti-discriminatory practice: Equality, diversity and social justice*. Bloomsbury Publishing.

Thornton III, G. C., and Byham, W. C. (2013). *Assessment centers and managerial performance*. Elsevier.

Trevino, L. K., Weaver, G. R., Gibson, D. G., and Toffler, B. L. (2014). Managing ethics and legal compliance: What works and what hurts. *Business Ethics Quarterly*, 24(2), 229–257. https://doi.org/10.5840/beq201424216.

Tuka, A. S. (2022). *Effective Keys to Employability and Entrepreneurship*. Ukiyoto Publishing.

Turner, P. (2019). *Employee engagement in contemporary organizations: Maintaining high productivity and sustained competitiveness.* Springer Nature.

Vanamali, S. (2023). *Personality Development and Communication Skills.* Academic Guru Publishing House.

Vardarlier, P. (2020). Digital transformation of human resource management: digital applications and strategic tools in HRM. *Digital business strategies in blockchain ecosystems: Transformational design and future of global business,* 239–264.

Wanberg, C. R., Ali, A. A., and Csillag, B. (2020). Job seeking: The process and experience of looking for a job. *Annual Review of Organizational Psychology and Organizational Behavior, 7,* 315–337.

Wang, Q., Hackett, R. D., Zhang, Y., and Cui, X. (2020). Personal characteristics and applicants' perceptions of procedural fairness in a selection context: The mediating role of procedural fairness expectations. *Management Decision, 58*(4), 687–704.

Wang, Q., and Liu, C. (2020). *Increasing market visibility through recruitment agencies. Journal of Career Advancement,* 18(3), 205–220.

Webster, D. (2021). *Ebook: Creating Adaptable Teams: From the Psychology of Coaching to the Practice of Leaders.* McGraw-Hill Education (UK).

Whitmore, T. (2017). *How to Write an Impressive CV and Cover Letter: A Comprehensive Guide for Jobseekers.* Hachette UK.

Wood, P. (2012). *SNAP: Making the most of first impressions, body language, and charisma.* New World Library.

Woods, A., and Tharakan, S. (2021). *Hiring for diversity: The guide to building an inclusive and equitable organization.* John Wiley and Sons.

World Health Organization. (2021). *WHO guideline on health workforce development, attraction, recruitment and retention in rural and remote areas:* web annexes.

Zairi, M. (2012). *Measuring performance for business results.* Springer Science and Business Media.

Zaychenko, I., Bagaeva, I., Smirnova, A., and Mutalieva, B. (2020). Digital transformation model of the staff selection system. In *Proceedings of the International Scientific Conference-Digital Transformation on Manufacturing, Infrastructure and Service* (pp. 1–6).

Zhu, C., Zhu, H., Xiong, H., Ma, C., Xie, F., Ding, P., and Li, P. (2018). Person-job fit: Adapting the right talent for the right job with joint representation learning. *ACM Transactions on Management Information Systems (TMIS)*, *9*(3), 1–17.

Zhang, L., and Yencha, C. (2022). Examining perceptions towards hiring algorithms. *Technology in Society, 68*, 101848.

www.ingramcontent.com/pod-product-compliance
Lightning Source LLC
Chambersburg PA
CBHW040753220326
41597CB00029BA/4770